j372.64
PER   Perry, Phyllis Jean.

Exploring the world
of sports.

$24.00

DATE			

Literature Bridges to Social Studies Series

Exploring the World of Sports: Linking Fiction to Nonfiction. By Phyllis J. Perry. 1998.

Exploring Our Country's History: Linking Fiction to Nonfiction. By Phyllis J. Perry. 1998.

Exploring the World of Sports

Linking Fiction to Nonfiction

Phyllis J. Perry

1998
Teacher Ideas Press
A Division of
Libraries Unlimited, Inc.
Englewood, Colorado

For my swimming companions,
Jay, *Jill*, and *David*

TEACHER IDEAS PRESS
A Division of
Libraries Unlimited, Inc.
P.O. Box 6633
Englewood, CO 80155-6633
1-800-237-6124
www.lu.com/tip

Production Editor: Kay Mariea
Copy Editor: Jason Cook
Proofreader: Cherie Rayburn
Typesetter: Kay Minnis

Library of Congress Cataloging-in-Publication Data

Perry, Phyllis Jean.
    Exploring the world of sports : linking fiction to nonfiction /
Phyllis J. Perry.
    xvi, 133 p. 22x28 cm. -- (Literature bridges to social studies series)
    ISBN 1-56308-570-4
    1. Sports literature--Study and teaching (Elementary) 2. Sports--
Study and teaching (Elementary) 3. Language arts--Correlation with
content subjects. 4. Interdisciplinary approach in education.
5. Education, Elementary--Activity programs. I. Title.
II. Series.
LB1575.P467   1998
372.64--dc21   97-43558
                                                      CIP

Contents

Part II
BASKETBALL

Part III
FOOTBALL

● **FICTION** (*continued*)

◆ **BRIDGES AND POETRY** 75

■ **NONFICTION CONNECTIONS** 79

Part IV
SOCCER, SWIMMING, TRACK AND FIELD

Part V
ADDITIONAL RESOURCES

About the Series

In this era of literature-based reading programs, students are involved in reading narratives more than ever before, but they still face difficulty when confronted with expository text. Many experts believe that one of the best ways to teach any topic is to engage the learner, that is, to interest students enough so that their motivation to learn about a topic increases.

The Literature Bridges to Social Studies series seeks to use the power of fiction to bring students from the world of imagination into the world of fact. In this series, fiction is used to build interest, increase familiarity with a topic, enlarge background, and introduce vocabulary. The fiction is to be enjoyed, letting the power of the story create a desire to learn more about a topic. A variety of fiction titles is used with the class, to suit individual tastes and the breadth of experience in a group of students.

As student interest builds naturally, one or more "bridge" books are used to pique interest in a topical exploration. At this point, the teacher can introduce a main theme of study to the class with confidence that students have developed sufficient background knowledge of that topic. Interest in the topic might then be strong enough to motivate students to attempt the expository writing in nonfiction titles.

Just as a variety of fiction titles should be used to introduce a topic, the Literature Bridges to Social Studies series suggests that a variety of nonfiction titles be offered to students as they begin their topical explorations. Thus, the series is particularly useful to those teachers who are transforming their teaching style to a cross-curricular approach. Nonfiction titles selected for this resource represent the more literary treatments of a topic, in contrast to a textbook-like stream of facts.

Introduction

This book is designed to assist any busy elementary teacher in planning an integrated unit of study involving sports. It includes suggestions for individual, small-group, and large-group activities across disciplines. Multiple titles allow for choice based on students' interests and skill levels. The titles, of various lengths and levels of difficulty, were selected from a large number of books recommended by children's librarians. This book is appropriate for teachers of kindergarten through fifth grade.

Between the fiction and nonfiction titles in each part are two suggested "bridge" titles. Bridge titles combine factual information with elements of narrative. They may also include interesting anecdotes and diary entries. This blend enables the reader to make an easy transition from fiction to nonfiction. Also included with the bridge titles is an appropriate book of sports poetry.

Parts I, II, III, and IV contain summaries of fiction titles, bridge and poetry titles, and nonfiction titles. For each fiction book, discussion starters and multidisciplinary activities are suggested. For each nonfiction title, topics for further investigation are suggested. These activities involve skills in research, oral and written language, science, math, geography, and the arts.

Each of these parts begins with a "bookweb," which lists all titles included in that part and suggests a variety of related topics to explore. All titles selected for this resource were published since 1980, the majority since 1990; and all are readily available. They represent many cultures and include many genres.

📖 Teaching Methods 📖

This book is designed to be used in a variety of teaching situations. It can be used by one teacher who is responsible for teaching a number of subjects to a group of students, by teachers in schools where there is departmentalization, and in team teaching situations.

One Teacher with Multiple Teaching Responsibilities

In most cases at the elementary level, a single teacher is responsible for teaching a variety of subjects to a group of students. If the same teacher is responsible for teaching language arts, social studies, math, and science, the multidisciplinary approach suggested in this book will have a unifying effect on the curriculum.

Before beginning a unit on sports, the teacher might, for example, read aloud one of the fiction titles in class. This will help set the tone for the upcoming unit of study. As students hear an interesting work of literature dealing with some aspect of sports, they will begin to learn the related vocabulary and to focus on their interest in sports.

The teacher might suggest that students be alert to information about sports and sports figures. Students might be encouraged to bring to class sports-related articles that they clip from newspapers and magazines for the beginnings of a classroom vertical file. If a scheduled television special will focus on some aspect of sports, such as the Super Bowl or the National Basketball Association (NBA) championship games, the teacher or another student might alert the class to the viewing opportunity.

Once the unit of study begins, the teacher might have each student select one of the fiction titles in Part I and then encourage small-group discussions and sharing among those who have read the same book. This will extend reading, listening, and speaking skills.

For the bridge titles, the teacher might want to assist students who are not as comfortable with nonfiction as they are with fiction. Because bridge titles combine elements of narrative or real-life adventure with nonfiction information and facts, they help students make the transition from one type of reading to the other. Students' growing vocabulary and knowledge about the world of sports will increase their interest in and appreciation of nonfiction.

In an expository writing assignment, the teacher might assign a writing topic related to sports and combine this with a math assignment for the students to compute (for example, the percentage of shots made from the free-throw line). In this way, a student will develop skills in researching, writing an informative paper (that explains, for example, the layout of a professional basketball court), and preparing a bibliography (if appropriate).

In a creative writing assignment, a student might write an original piece from the point of view of a young baseball player who surprises everyone by hitting a home run during an important game. A creative writing assignment is an excellent opportunity to introduce sports poetry. Students might experiment with writing their own poetry after reading a collection included in this resource.

Depending upon the books selected, the teacher might combine social studies with geography. For example, as students learn about the time in our history when baseball was segregated, a topic presented in the book *Leagues Apart: The Men and Times of the Negro Baseball Leagues*, they might locate the cities where Negro Baseball League games were played; or they might locate on a U.S. map the regions most effected by the Dust Bowl, a topic presented in the book *Cat Running* (Part IV).

Departmentalization with Team Planning

In schools where departmentalization is combined with team planning time, the language arts, social studies, math, and science teachers responsible for students in the primary or intermediate grades might plan a segment of time for a unit on sports. The math teacher might concentrate on helping students understand such sports topics as batting averages, earned run averages, and dimensions of playing fields. The social studies teacher might discuss desegregation in professional sports and the obstacles early pioneers like Jackie Robinson had to face, or baseball games played in the internment camps to which Japanese Americans were confined during World War II. The language arts teacher might assign reading, research, and writing assignments based on both fiction and nonfiction titles. Panel discussions and oral presentations of material will improve speaking and listening skills. Specific skills such as skimming, reading for information, note taking, outlining, and using an index or a glossary of terms might also be introduced or reinforced using nonfiction titles.

Some students will find it easy to understand factual information pictorially or in graphs and charts in nonfiction titles. For other students, these may be new sources of information. The teacher should explain how to "read" numerical data and might design assignments so that students will have an opportunity to construct their own tables and graphs.

Specialists in the school might also be involved. The music teacher might incorporate some sports songs. The art teacher might have students sculpt sports figures using clay or soft, flexible wire to create the illusion of figures in motion. Classroom and hallway bulletin boards might feature a sport that is currently in season or an international event, such as the Olympic Games. The physical education teacher can also contribute to this unit of study.

If the school has a computer lab, sports-related software and other media might be purchased, such as Sports Illustrated's *Multimedia Sports Almanac*, an interactive encyclopedia for CD-ROM. Students might write their reports for this unit of study using word processing software.

If the media specialist is responsible for teaching research skills to students, the focus might be on using an interactive encyclopedia on CD-ROM that features a particular sport, using a vertical file on sports heroes, or searching a software database on the origins of a sport. The media specialist might designate an "interest center" for videos, magazines, and books in the media center's collection that feature sports, or use interlibrary loans to increase the materials available for this unit of study.

Team Teaching

Where team teaching occurs, the various team members might choose to present their favorite lessons and experiments based on personal expertise or interest in a new topic. Next, teachers might map a sequence and timeline so that their students will see the connections among their various subject areas. While one teacher is presenting a lesson, colleagues might assist with small-group discussions, science experiments, or supervision in the media center of a group of students involved in small-group or individual research.

Some activities, such as the showing of films or videos, might be presented to a large group of students. The team members might be responsible for group stations, in which smaller numbers of students are given the opportunity to extend their knowledge.

📖 Culminating Activities 📖

Whatever the configuration of students and teachers, a special culminating activity can be prepared for each part of this unit of study. Part IV, for example, deals with soccer, swimming, and track and field, so as a culminating activity, students might plan and manage a grade-level track and field day.

Finding a time in the school schedule to hold the event; securing the cooperation of all teachers involved, including the physical education teacher; determining which events to include; planning a schedule of events; creating a registration system for students to enter the events; writing permission slips to be sent home with students; writing invitations to parents; arranging for snacks and beverages; planning a first-aid center; securing adult volunteers to help in judging and timing; setting up equipment; securing trophies or ribbons (some of which might be donated); and so on will provide ample opportunities for student committees to contribute.

Different culminating activities will come to mind as students become immersed in their reading. For example, as a culminating activity for Part I, students might form committees, plan a budget, and make arrangements for taking the entire class on an imaginary trip. Perhaps they'd like to attend a World Series game. How much would round-trip plane fare cost? What would it cost to charter a bus, and what would be the best route of travel? What lodging is available at what rates? How much money should be allowed per student for the cost of food, tickets, and entertainment at the game? In this example, students would need to use language arts, mathematics, and geography skills.

📖 Scope and Sequence 📖

The fiction and nonfiction titles included in this resource emphasize that girls as well as boys are actively involved in sports, that sports greats are found in all ethnic groups, and that people with disabilities and health problems can actively participate in sports.

Part I covers baseball. The fiction titles include picture books and chapter books. Each book deals with some aspect of baseball. The nonfiction titles discuss such baseball topics as tips for becoming a better player; great hitters; collecting baseball cards; tee-ball; and baseball greats, including Hank Aaron, Josh Gibson, and Jose Canseco.

Part II covers basketball. The fiction titles include picture books and chapter books. The nonfiction titles discuss such basketball topics as developing game skills; making the team; and basketball greats, including Larry Bird, Michael Jordan, and Shaquille O'Neal.

Part III covers football. The fiction titles include picture books and chapter books. The nonfiction titles discuss such football topics as winners of the Heisman Trophy; the various positions on the team; and football greats, including Joe Namath, Joe Montana, and Steve Young.

Part IV covers soccer, swimming, and track and field. The fiction titles include picture books and chapter books. The nonfiction titles discuss such topics as soccer techniques, synchronized swimming, scuba diving, and track's magnificent milers.

Part V is a list of additional resources. Included are additional fiction and nonfiction titles for baseball; basketball; football; and soccer, swimming, and track and field.

Part I
Baseball

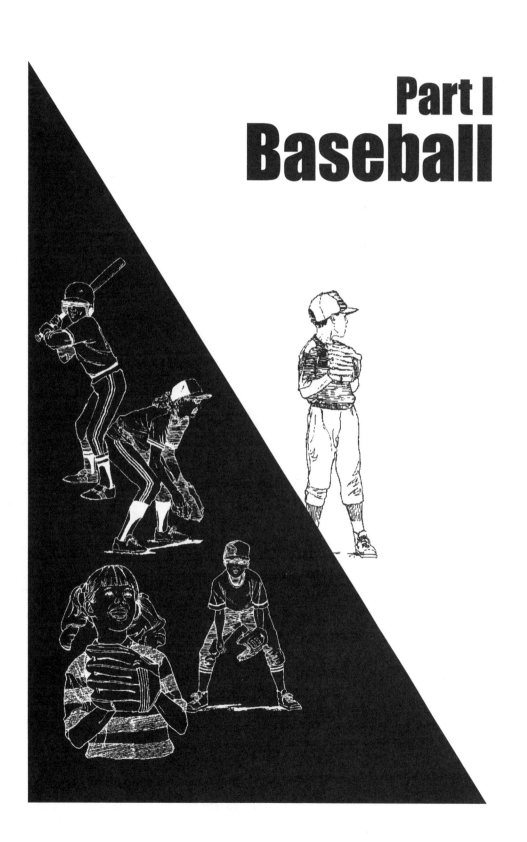

Baseball

● FICTION ●

- 📖 *Albert's Ballgame*
- 📖 *Baseball Card Crazy*
- 📖 *Baseball Saved Us*
- 📖 *Coco Grimes*
- 📖 *Ghost Dog*
- 📖 *The Hit-Away Kid*

- 📖 *How Georgie Radbourn Saved Baseball*
- 📖 *Mayfield Crossing*
- 📖 *My Dad's Baseball*
- 📖 *The Toilet Paper Tigers*
- 📖 *Zero's Slider*

◆ BRIDGES AND POETRY ◆

- 📖 *Baseball Kids*
- 📖 *Batboy: An Inside Look at Spring Training*
- 📖 *At the Crack of the Bat*

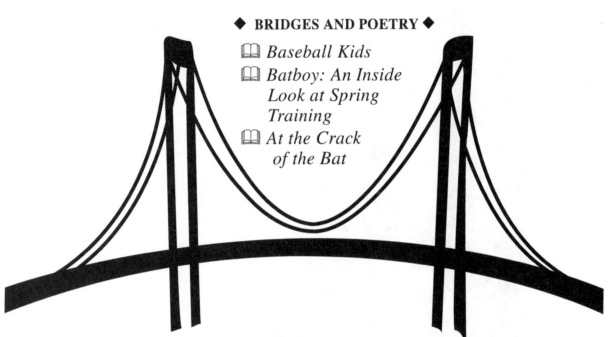

■ NONFICTION CONNECTIONS ■

- 📖 *Baseball's Greatest Hitters*
- 📖 *Belles of the Ballpark*
- 📖 *Everyone Wins at Tee-Ball*
- 📖 *The Great American Baseball Strike*
- 📖 *Hank Aaron*
- 📖 *The Illustrated Rules of Baseball*

- 📖 *Jackie Robinson Breaks the Color Line*
- 📖 *Jose Canseco: Baseball Superstar, Famous Record Breaker*
- 📖 *Josh Gibson: Baseball Great*
- 📖 *A Kid's Guide to Collecting Baseball Cards*
- 📖 *Leagues Apart: The Men and Times of the Negro Baseball Leagues*

—OTHER TOPICS TO EXPLORE—

—announcing	—baseballs	—pennants	—wiffle ball
—base running	—coaches	—signals	—wood for bats
—baseball camps	—mascots	—umpire schools	—World Series

From *Exploring the World of Sports*. © 1998 Phyllis J. Perry. Teacher Ideas Press. (800) 237-6124.

● *Fiction* ●

📖 *Albert's Ballgame*

📖 *Baseball Card Crazy*

📖 *Baseball Saved Us*

📖 *Coco Grimes*

📖 *Ghost Dog*

📖 *The Hit-Away Kid*

📖 *How Georgie Radbourn Saved Baseball*

📖 *Mayfield Crossing*

📖 *My Dad's Baseball*

📖 *The Toilet Paper Tigers*

📖 *Zero's Slider*

📖 *Albert's Ballgame*

FICTION

written and illustrated by Leslie Tryon

New York: Atheneum Books for Young Readers, 1996. 40p. (unnumbered)

This colorfully illustrated book will appeal to students in kindergarten and first grade.

The book begins by explaining to readers that when it is springtime in Pleasant Valley, everyone who is anyone goes out to the Old Field to play ball. The pictures show that everyone in Pleasant Valley is an animal, including Albert, a big, white duck who is the manager of a baseball team called the Pleasant Valley Ducks.

Through action-filled pictures, accompanied by minimal text, the reader learns how various animals pitch—bean balls and mean balls, knuckle balls and chuckle balls, and sometimes even inside balls. As the balls come over the plate, the batters hit fly balls, sky balls, slow balls, toe balls, and foul balls.

Many other kinds of balls are featured at the game, including balls that fall into horns of musicians or into outstretched baseball caps; popcorn balls; balls of ice cream; and ball-like, sticky candied apples.

Spectators play with beach balls while the players catch stray balls, curve balls, swerve balls, and sometimes manage to collide with one another and miss the ball altogether. Even a ball-shaped hot-air balloon makes an appearance at the game.

Sometimes the players hit a home run; sometimes they walk, steal, or slide into base. The scoreboard shows that one team wins and the other team loses.

Discussion Starters and Multidisciplinary Activities

1   Many animals are pictured in this book. Some are common and familiar while others are unusual. Have students take turns pointing out and identifying a favorite animal from the book. Are there any they can't identify?

2   Ask students whether the A team or the B team won the game. How many innings did they play? Invite students to explain how they came up with their answers, based on pictures from the book.

3   Readers will become fond of the character Albert. Have available at a classroom "interest center" other Albert books by Leslie Tryon for children to read, such as *Albert's Alphabet, Albert's Play, Albert's Field Trip, Albert's Thanksgiving,* and *One Gaping Wide-Mouthed Hopping Frog.*

4   On a classroom bulletin board, draw two baseball diamonds. Label one field "The As" and the other field "The Bs." Have students draw pictures of the 21 animals depicted in the book and position them appropriately on the two playing fields. To determine which animal should appear where, have students use the chart on the last page of the book. (There are nine animals for each team, plus the manager, the home-base umpire, and the bat rabbit.)

5   Invite students to name several animals that are not pictured in the book. Have students draw one of these animals and write a short narrative that describes it, identifies the position it might play on a baseball team, and explains why the animal would excel in this position.

6   Ask students to come up with another ball that might have appeared at Albert's ballgame and draw a picture that shows this new ball at the game.

FICTION

📖 *Baseball Card Crazy*

by Trish Kennedy and Timothy Schodorf
New York: Charles Scribner's Sons, 1993. 72p.

This book will appeal to readers in grades three through five. It is not illustrated.

The central character, Oliver O'Malley, has the best baseball card collection of anyone in his fifth-grade class at Millard Fillmore Elementary School. Oliver believes that he could have the best collection of cards in the entire state of Ohio if only he could find the cards that his father collected as a boy.

Oliver's father explains that he had some great cards, but he doesn't know what happened to them. When Oliver's parents decide to leave him and his sister with their grandparents for three weeks, Oliver decides that he will make good use of his time there on the farm by searching for his father's old baseball cards.

Oliver and his grandmother search the attic but only find some of Oliver's father's old clothes, which Oliver resists trying on. Oliver searches the basement and finds his father's old bookbag and some of his father's school papers, but no cards.

Oliver and his grandfather hunt for an old clubhouse on the property—Oliver is sure that he will find the cards there. They find the clubhouse, but even though it's a great old building, Oliver doesn't find the cards.

Oliver gives up his search and enjoys his time on the farm, playing with a friend in the old clubhouse. Then, just before Oliver is to return home, he tries on the old clothes from the attic. In the pockets of his dad's old jacket, Oliver finds the precious cards for which he's been searching.

Discussion Starters and Multidisciplinary Activities

1   Oliver thinks that his little sister, Samantha, is a pain, yet throughout the story, he's very patient with her. Have students discuss the relationship between Oliver and Sam.

2   Oliver's grandparents demonstrate in many ways throughout the book that they know how to get along with and please children. Have students find instances in the text that show how the grandparents and children interact.

3   Many students in the class will have something that has been handed down to them from parents, grandparents, or other relatives. It might be a watch, a doll, or a baseball glove. Allow time for students to discuss these items and why they value them.

4   With the help of a media specialist, obtain a copy of *Baseball Card Weekly* to share with the class. Students can see what aspect of card collecting is featured each week and learn how dealers and collectors use this resource to price baseball cards.

5   Oliver's father and grandfather use a lot of colloquial expressions, such as the idiom "There's more than one way to skin a cat." Have a group of students make a list of colloquial expressions they know and post the list in the classroom. Have other students in the class add to the list.

6   Invite students to write an original short story about a topic of their choice. Have students conclude the story with an expression appropriate for the situation. The expression might be taken from the list written for activity 5 (above), or students may want to write an original expression. Have students share their stories with the class.

 ## *Baseball Saved Us*

FICTION

by Ken Mochizuki
illustrated by Dom Lee
New York: Lee & Low Books, 1993. 32p. (unnumbered)

Older primary students will enjoy this picture book, realistically illustrated in soft, sepia tones. It tells the story of people of Japanese descent who were placed in internment camps away from the West Coast during World War II.

The story is told from the viewpoint of a Japanese boy who has been sent to an internment camp. The camp is unpleasant—hot in the daytime and cold at night. The boy's father decides to build a baseball field to give people something to do.

Together, the people create a ballfield. They funnel water from irrigation ditches to flood the field, and they pack down the soil to make it hard. Friends back in California send them bats, balls, and gloves. The women sew uniforms. When everything is ready, the adults and the children play ball. The narrator practices hard and plays second base on his team. Other players tease him and call "easy out" when he comes up to bat.

In one of the last games of the year to decide the championship, the boy is up to bat in the bottom of the ninth inning, with two outs. He hits a home run. The others carry him around like a hero on their shoulders. Even the man in the tower who is guarding the camp gives him a "thumbs up" sign.

When the boy returns to his home in California, he has no friends. During baseball season, he makes the school team. Some fans call him a "Jap" and cheer against him, but he keeps playing and hits another home run.

Discussion Starters and Multidisciplinary Activities

1 The boy's father and the boy's older brother, Teddy, have an argument early in the book when Teddy refuses to get his father a drink of water. Ask the students to discuss why they think Teddy has changed and is now so rude to his father.

2 Twice during this book, the narrator is a hero. Have the students discuss if they think the boy felt proudest during his moment as a hero in the internment camp or during his moment as a hero when he was back at school. Why?

3 The boy in the book has the nickname Shorty. Some people like their nicknames; other people hate them. Invite students to discuss nicknames. What might you do if people began calling you by a nickname that you hated?

4 The book's jacket states that the author was born in Seattle, Washington; that the author's parents were sent during World War II to the Minidoka internment camp in Idaho; and that the illustrator grew up in Seoul, South Korea. Have two students research these locations and point them out on a map to their classmates.

5 In an author's note, the reader learns that in 1988, the U.S. government admitted that putting people of Japanese descent into internment camps during World War II was wrong. Have a group of students, with the help of a media specialist, research the government's apology. Have the students share with the class what they learn.

6 The hero of the book is in at least two big games. Have interested students try to capture the excitement of a big baseball game by writing a poem titled "The Big Game."

FICTION

📖 *Coco Grimes*

by Mary Stolz
New York: HarperCollins, 1994. 90p.

This easy-to-read chapter book will appeal to readers in grades two through four. The story is told in the third person from the viewpoint of Thomas, a young baseball fan who lives with his grandfather.

Thomas is about to celebrate his birthday. His grandfather tells him that, in addition to a family birthday party, Thomas will get to go to a baseball game. The old truck barely gets them there and back, but Thomas and his grandfather have a wonderful day at the ballpark. A man sitting behind Thomas catches a fly ball and gives it to Thomas in honor of his birthday. The ball was hit by one of Thomas's heroes, Bobby Bonilla.

Thomas learns that a man who once played in the Negro leagues, now in his 90s, lives in Miami. Grandfather's friend Milo McCallam suggests that they visit the old player, Coco Grimes, and talk with him. Because he fears his old truck won't make the trip, Grandfather borrows a car for the weekend.

They drive to see Mr. McCallam at a motel where he lives. The next day, while Grandfather goes fishing, Thomas interviews Coco. He has a confusing talk with the old man, who sometimes forgets who he is talking to and sometimes gets angry. Thomas also gets to see his aunt who takes him to a raree, or fair, where she wins a prize for quickly solving a jigsaw puzzle.

Thomas and his grandfather return home. They have enjoyed the trip but are happy to be back in familiar surroundings.

Discussion Starters and Multidisciplinary Activities

1 Grandfather sometimes makes up words to convey his unique ideas. For example, on page 23, he talks about the *volumptuous* night sounds. Ask students to define what they think grandfather meant when he used this word. Ask students to make up and define a word to describe the sounds they might hear on a summer evening.

2 Grandfather suggests that Thomas end each diary entry with the phrase "and so to bed," following the style of a journal keeper named Samuel Pepys. Have a group of three interested students research Samuel Pepys and find out what made him famous. Have the students share with the class what they learn.

3 Have students discuss why Thomas found his interview with Coco Grimes confusing. Was the interview successful? Why?

4 Coco tells Thomas about Jackie Robinson breaking into the major league white teams. Ask a pair of interested students to research this topic. When did Jackie Robinson break into the majors? For what team did he play? Did he set any records?

5 The author of this book, Mary Stolz, wrote two novels that were named Newbery Honor Books. Have interested students, with the help of a media specialist, research this honor. Have them share with the class what they learn.

6 The sunset over the Gulf is described as the color of Gatorade. Have two students, with help from a media specialist, research light and refraction. How are the colors seen in a sunset over water produced? Have the students share the information with the class.

 *Ghost Dog*

FICTION

by Ellen Leroe
illustrated by Bill Basso
New York: Hyperion Books for Children, 1993. 64p.

This book will appeal to second- through third-grade readers. It is illustrated with humorous black-and-white drawings.

The central character, Artie Jensen, visits Grandpa Noonie's new house. Immediately, Artie finds that the house is haunted—by a dog that no one except Artie can see. This ghost dog is a short, fat, wrinkly faced pug.

Grandpa Noonie offers Artie a ticket to a baseball card show and gives him a 1967 Tom Seaver card to trade or sell. Ghost Dog follows Artie into a book and card shop. Artie shows off his baseball card and learns that it's worth $1,000.

A man who claims to be a newspaper reporter wanting to write a story about Artie leads them to the newspaper office. The man disappears with the card, and Artie soon learns that he is not a reporter on the staff. Artie realizes that he has been conned.

Artie continues to the card show, where the thief is holding up Artie's baseball card. Ghost Dog takes action: He rushes through the crowd, bites the thief, and runs off with the card.

Security guards come to investigate. The thief snatches the card and tries to escape, but Ghost Dog again retrieves the card.

Back at Grandpa's house, Ghost Dog makes Artie look good by catching a fly ball in a backyard game. When Artie gets in the car to go home, he is happy to find that Ghost Dog is coming home with him.

Discussion Starters and Multidisciplinary Activities

1 Have students discuss why they think Grandpa Noonie met his visitors wearing a funny rubber nose that made him look like a pig.

2 Although Artie says he doesn't like his two older cousins, Homer and Socko, he keeps trying to impress them. Have students discuss why they think Artie does this.

3 Artie's mother thinks that Artie invented Ghost Dog because he's trying to convince her to buy him a pet. If Artie continues to have these adventures, will Mom eventually buy a real dog for him? If so, will Ghost Dog disappear? Have students discuss this.

4 Artie describes his made-up comic book, "The Adventures of Dino Boy." Dino Boy is half boy and half dinosaur. Have a small group of interested students write one or more original comic book adventures featuring Dino Boy. Have them share their creations with the class.

5 Someone in the class might have a baseball card collection and might be willing to show a few cards to the class. Have the student explain what determines the value that the cards have. (Keep the cards in a safe place before and after the sharing time.)

6 Certain magazines and sites on the World Wide Web specialize in providing information on the current values of baseball cards. Have a group of students, with the help of a media specialist, make a list of magazines and Web sites that provide information about baseball cards. Have the students share this information with the class.

 *The Hit-Away Kid*

FICTION

by Matt Christopher
illustrated by George Ulrich
Boston: Little, Brown, 1988. 60p.

This easy-to-read chapter book will appeal to second- and third-grade readers. There are 10 short chapters, each of which includes a black-and-white drawing.

The story is told from the viewpoint of Barry McGee, a left fielder on the Peach Street Mudders baseball team. Barry enjoys being called a "hit-away batter" by the fans. Barry gets his glove under a long fly ball and makes a great catch, but the ball rolls out of his glove. Thinking no one has seen this, Barry jumps up shouting, "I've got it!"

Barry's sister, Susan, sees him drop the ball. She talks to him about his cheating. That night at supper, Barry confesses to his parents what he did but promises not to cheat again.

While Barry and Susan are out skateboarding, Susan drops a small figurine from her pocket. It is a special Disneyland souvenir belonging to their younger brother. The pitcher from the High Street Bunkers, Alec Frost, picks up the figurine and refuses to return it. He vows to strike out Barry in their next game but promises to return the figurine if Barry hits two home runs.

At the game, Barry strikes out once, hits a home run, and gets another hit but fails to touch second base. He confesses that he missed the base and allows himself to be tagged out. The Mudders lose, but Alec Frost congratulates Barry, and Barry learns that a person can change and learn to do the right thing.

Discussion Starters and Multidisciplinary Activities

1   Barry ignores orders from his coach about bunting and about base running. His coach isn't happy, and he tells Barry that he must play by the same rules as everybody else. Have students discuss whether they think the coach was fair with Barry. What is the coach's role in building team spirit?

2   Susan promises not to tell her parents how Barry cheated, pretending that he caught a fly ball he had really dropped. She says, "It's your problem, not mine." Have students discuss if they would have handled this situation the same way Susan did or differently.

3   At the end of the book, Barry tells his coach that he missed second base. Alec returns the figurine even though Barry didn't hit two home runs. Have students discuss which of these actions they admire most. Why?

4   Ask students to study and clip at least two short articles from the local newspaper's sports section during a particular week. Have them read aloud to classmates colorful verbs used to describe the game, such as "*knocked* out three hits," "*nabbed* a fly ball," and "*edged* the other team."

5   Have interested students write an original short story about one inning of a baseball game. What nicknames will the players have? Is there plenty of action? Post the stories on a classroom bulletin board.

6   The story ends with Barry and Susan racing home to return the figurine to their little brother. Invite interested students to make an illustration for this page using any medium they prefer. Post the pictures on a classroom bulletin board.

From *Exploring the World of Sports*. © 1998 Phyllis J. Perry. Teacher Ideas Press. (800) 237-6124.

📖 *How Georgie Radbourn Saved Baseball*

FICTION

by David Shannon
New York: Blue Sky Press, 1994. 32p. (unnumbered)

This book will appeal to students in kindergarten through third grade. It includes full-page illustrations in muted colors. The story combines elements of a contemporary political cartoon, a fairy tale, and a tall tale.

As the story opens, people in the United States are enjoying four seasons of the year, and baseball is a national pastime. Then a ballplayer named Boss Swaggert falls into a slump, strikes out in a critical game, and vows not to play ball again.

When Boss Swaggert becomes rich and powerful, he convinces the public to abolish baseball. He throws ballplayers into prison, confiscates baseball equipment, and bulldozes the ballparks. In place of ballparks, he builds factories, for which he maintains a force of factory police. He forbids anyone to use baseball sayings. It is now unseasonably cold all year long.

Ebbet and Mary Radbourn have high hopes for their baby, Georgie, who is born in April. As Georgie grows, though, his parents begin to worry about him. Forbidden baseball sayings keep popping out of his mouth. Georgie also throws snowballs at factory police.

After Georgie goes to work in a factory, he is arrested for shouting a baseball phrase, and he is tried before Boss Swaggert. Georgie's lawyer proposes that if Georgie can strike out Boss Swaggert, Georgie will be free and baseball will again become the national pastime. When Boss strikes out, the clouds part, the sun comes out, and everyone begins to play ball.

Discussion Starters and Multidisciplinary Activities

1 Some of the illustrations in this book resemble political cartoons. Invite students to clip political cartoons from local newspapers and bring them to class. Discuss how certain features are exaggerated in the cartoons.

2 To protect Georgie from the factory police, his parents wrap him up before he goes to work in the factory, so he will be unable to talk. Ask students what other techniques the parents might have used to protect their son.

3 Baseball phrases are forbidden by Boss Swaggert. Have students brainstorm and list as many baseball phrases as they can. In the context of a game, what do these phrases mean? Have students suggest other contexts in which these phrases might have different meanings.

4 Have a group of students, with the help of a media specialist, research the weather in your town. What is the average daytime temperature for each month of the year? What is the difference between the average daytime temperatures of the hottest month and the coldest month? Have students share this information with the class.

5 On the chalkboard, help the students create a class graph of favorite sports. Number the vertical axis from 0 to 20; list a variety of sports along the horizontal axis. Fill in the graph to show how many students consider baseball, basketball, soccer, and so forth their favorite sport.

6 Some sports, such as baseball, require special equipment. Invite to class an adult who can bring and share such items as a catcher's mask, the protective padded vests and shin guards that catchers wear, various mitts and gloves, bats, and so on.

📖 *Mayfield Crossing*

FICTION

by Vaunda Micheaux Nelson
New York: G. P. Putnam's Sons, 1993. 88p.

This book will appeal to readers in grades three through five. It is illustrated with a few black-and-white drawings.

Mayfield Crossing is a special place where all the neighborhood children know one another, play ball together, and attend school at Mayfield Schoolhouse.

All the children are excited and a little afraid when their old schoolhouse is boarded up and they learn that this year they will go by bus to attend Parkview Elementary. Meg and the others learn that it will not be easy at the new school.

Some students and staff do not welcome the new children and are especially insensitive to those who are black. In the lunchroom, in the classrooms, and on the playground, the Mayfield students are met with prejudice. When one of the Parkview boys knocks Meg down, and her brother, Billie, gets in a fight to protect her, the three children are sent to the principal's office. The principal tries to get at the root of the problem and deals fairly with all three children.

Meg and Billie don't know how to change things at school. They decide to hold a championship baseball game pitting the Mayfield kids against the Parkview students. It looks as if the Mayfield students will have to forfeit the game, but Ivy, a Parkview student, saves the day by playing on the Mayfield team, saying that they are all Parkview students. As the story ends, it looks as if the new children may be accepted.

Discussion Starters and Multidisciplinary Activities

1 The character Hairy doesn't actually do much in the story, and yet he manages to play a major role. Have students discuss why they think the author included Hairy in this story.

2 Have the students discuss the Parkview principal, Mr. Callahan, and what they think he said to Meg and Billie's parents when he phoned to tell them about the fight. How would he present what happened?

3 Ivy plays a small but important role in the story. She changes from refusing to have anything to do with the Mayfield children to helping them by playing on their baseball team. Ask students to discuss why they think Ivy changes.

4 The outcome of the important championship game is not given in the story. Ask interested students to write Chapter Fourteen, describing the outcome of the baseball game. There should be several versions, with various outcomes. Share these stories aloud with the class and discuss them.

5 The fancy new car in this story is a Studebaker, which is no longer manufactured. Have a small group of students, with the help of a media specialist or an adult volunteer, research automobiles. When and where were Studebakers manufactured? When were the last Studebakers made? Have students share with the class what they learn.

6 None of the drawings show Hairy, but he is described in detail. Invite students to draw Hairy, using any medium they prefer. Post these drawings on a classroom bulletin board.

 ## *My Dad's Baseball*

FICTION

by Ron Cohen

New York: Lothrop, Lee & Shepard, 1994. 32p. (unnumbered)

Students from kindergarten through third grade will enjoy this story, told in the first person by a father to his seven-year-old son. The book contains half text and half full-page color pictures.

When a father, Ron, accidentally comes upon an old baseball, he tells his son about a special day, June 4, 1955. On that day, his father was taking him and his brother to their first baseball game to see the New York Yankees play the Detroit Tigers.

In Dad's family, everyone hates the Yankees, except for Aunt Ethel. Dad is a fan of the Milwaukee Braves and, especially, of Eddie Mathews. He wears a cap and carries his Eddie Mathews baseball card with him everywhere. Uncle Lenny arrives in his 1955 Dodge to give them a ride to the ballpark.

They look out over Yankee Stadium and then take seats in the lower right-field stands. Dad looks at Mickey Mantle through his binoculars and sees Mantle chewing gum and blowing bubbles. In the sixth inning, Yogi Berra hits a ball into the stands. When the ball sails over everyone's head and crashes into the stands, Dad comes up with it.

The next day, Uncle Lenny drives the boys back to the stadium so that they can ask Yogi to sign the baseball. Ron tries to hide the fact that he is a Braves fan, but his hat falls out of his pocket while he is talking to Yogi Berra. Yogi says, "You should always be who you are." He signs the ball and shakes hands with the boy. After telling the story, Dad gives the ball to his son.

Discussion Starters and Multidisciplinary Activities

1   In this story, a father tells a story of when he was a boy. At the end of the story, the father gives his son a souvenir—a baseball signed by Yogi Berra. Invite students to share with the class their favorite souvenirs.

2   Some students in the class will have favorite sports figures and teams. Some may have cards showing their sports heroes. Allow time for students to discuss their favorites.

3   To help evoke the time period of this story, the author mentions a brand-new 1955 Dodge. Some students in the class may be interested in old automobiles. Have a small group of students, with help from a media specialist, research cars of the 1950s and bring to class and share pictures of various models.

4   Dad admits that he liked the Milwaukee Braves because of their uniforms, which featured a Native American; a tomahawk; and the colors black, white, and red. Invite students to draw and color a logo for a new sports team. What should the name of the team be? What should the logo look like?

5   Mickey Mantle was one of Aunt Ethel's favorite ballplayers. Have a group of students, with the help of an adult volunteer or a media specialist, research Mickey Mantle. When did he play ball? Did he set any records? Have the students share with the class what they learn.

6   Some sports games begin with the playing of the national anthem; others have special songs associated with the game. Ask the vocal music teacher to teach the students sports songs, including "Take Me Out to the Ballgame."

The Toilet Paper Tigers

by Gordon Korman
New York: Scholastic, 1993. 195p.

FICTION

This humorous contemporary book will appeal to third- through fifth-grade readers. It is not illustrated.

Sixth-grader Corey Johnson hopes for a good season of little league baseball, but the coach, a kindly professor, knows nothing about the game. The uniforms have pictures of toilet paper on them, thanks to their sponsor, Feather Soft Bathroom Tissue, Inc. Then the professor's granddaughter, Kristy, filled with New York talk, arrives and begins bossing around the team. Because Kristy has snapped a potentially embarrassing photo of the boys in the locker room, they are forced to suffer her coaching.

One by one, using persistence and creativity, Kristy deals with the players. Luis Bono, the catcher, has to get over his fear of being smashed in the face with a ball. Tuba Dave, playing second base, has to lose weight so that he can run the bases. Ernie will have to quit the team unless he learns enough math to pass his tests. Right fielder Ryan Crisp needs help with all his jobs because he's falling asleep on the field. Caspar Howard has to transfer his skills at ice skating into base running. Tim Laredo needs help with his big brother. The Devereaux twins need a way to share one position on the team. The hero of the book, Corey Johnson, needs to find some way to show that he's a better pitcher than Kevin Featherstone.

Kristy eventually turns the players into a winning team. In the course of all this, the team members come to appreciate Kristy and her grandfather.

Discussion Starters and Multidisciplinary Activities

1 Because Kristy is audacious, she bluffs her way through many difficult situations. Ask students to describe incidents from the story and explain how Kristy gets through them.

2 The professor is what is called a stereotype. He plays the role of a scientist who is totally ignorant about baseball, as well as car engines. Have students discuss other stereotypes they have encountered in books or movies.

3 Ask students to discuss whether they were surprised at the end of the book to learn that Kristy was from Bedrock Dam, New York, instead of from New York City. Had any students suspected that she was not from the city? Why?

4 The Tigers entered the playoffs only because one of the four winning teams was stricken with mumps. Ask a pair of interested students to research mumps. What causes them? How can they be passed to someone else? What sort of treatment is necessary? Have students share with the class what they learn.

5 Having lepton power in a glass jar was a way to convince team members that they couldn't lose. Many people believe in some sort of lucky charm. A rabbit's foot is supposed to be lucky. Have students, with the help of a media specialist, research lucky charms. Have students share with the class what they learn.

6 Invite students to choose a scene from the book and illustrate it using any medium they prefer. They should write a caption that explains the scene depicted and note the page in the book where they would include the illustration. Post the pictures on a classroom bulletin board.

From *Exploring the World of Sports*. © 1998 Phyllis J. Perry. Teacher Ideas Press. (800) 237-6124.

 *Zero's Slider*

FICTION

by Matt Christopher
illustrated by Molly Delaney
New York: Little, Brown, 1994. 63p.

This book, with comical black-and-white illustrations, will appeal to first-through third-grade readers. It is part of a series of easy chapter books called Springboard Books.

The hero of the book, Zero Ford, pitches for the Peach Street Mudders. As the book opens, Zero is having a bad pitching day and is particularly unhappy because his Uncle Pete has come to watch the game. His uncle, an announcer, is job hunting.

Coach Parker suggests that Zero practice more during the upcoming week, but that night, Zero slams a door on a finger of his pitching hand. Zero's uncle uses ice to reduce the swelling and assures Zero that he will be pitching again in a few days.

When Zero does try pitching, he finds that he can throw a beautiful slider, which will be effective against opponents. Zero worries that once his finger has healed and the bandage has been removed, he may no longer be able to throw a slider. Meanwhile, Coach Parker is asking players to help him find someone to serve as a substitute coach for two weeks, so the team won't have to forfeit games while their coach is away.

When Zero removes the bandage, he can't throw a slider anymore. Still, his uncle says that he's throwing good pitches, and that's what counts. Uncle Pete agrees to coach the team for two weeks before leaving to accept a new job.

Discussion Starters and Multidisciplinary Activities

1 A pitcher and catcher have a special relationship in baseball. In this book, Zero and Chess have a special relationship off the field as well as on the field. Have students discuss the friendship between these two boys.

2 When Uncle Pete becomes angry while listening to an inept sports announcer, Zero is afraid to ask him to serve as a substitute coach. Have students discuss why they think Uncle Pete may be angrier and more on edge than usual.

3 Zero's ability to throw a pitch called a slider came and went quickly. Uncle Pete says that, some day, Zero will again be able to throw his "killer pitch." Have students discuss whether they agree that Zero's slider will return to him.

4 The story does not suggest how Zero Ford came to have such a strange name. Invite interested students to write a short story that explains how Zero came to have his name. Have students share their stories with the class.

5 Many pitchers have special pitches for which they are famous. One important pitch is the fast ball. Pitches are clocked in miles per hour. Ask a pair of students to research exactly how fast today's big league pitchers are throwing fast balls. Have the students share with the class what they learn.

6 An important pitching statistic is earned run average (ERA). Have a pair of students research the ERA of a pitcher they admire and then explain to the class how this statistic is calculated and interpreted.

 Bridges and Poetry

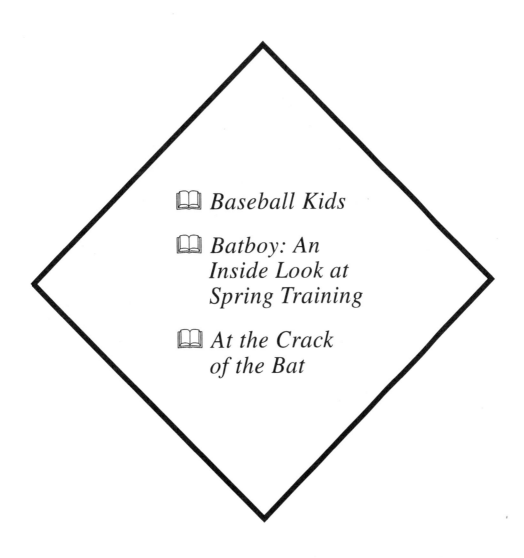

📖 *Baseball Kids*

📖 *Batboy: An Inside Look at Spring Training*

📖 *At the Crack of the Bat*

 *Baseball Kids*

by George Sullivan
New York: Cobblehill Books, 1990. 96p.

**BRIDGES
AND POETRY**

This book will appeal to third- through fifth-grade readers. It is illustrated with black-and-white photographs.

Each chapter in this book covers an interview with an eleven- or twelve-year-old boy who plays on a baseball team. The first interview is with Mike St. Clair, who plays as a pitcher and a shortstop. Pat Campbell talks about playing left field and third base and about overcoming fear at the plate to become a determined hitter with a fluid swing. Omar Ramirez describes playing second and third base as well as pitching; he has taught himself to bat, both right- and left-handed. Pat Hellyer tells about playing second base and catcher and about attending clinics at a baseball camp to improve bunting and base running.

Dan Desilets describes playing second base, as well as left and center field; although he prefers certain positions, he is versatile and willing to play wherever he can help his team. Brian Karavish not only plays first and third base but is also clean-up hitter for his team. Seneca Perez is a center fielder who practices often with his stepfather. Tom Mineo, an outstanding hitter, pitches and plays first base. Steven Mazzariello plays shortstop, second base, and pitcher; he began his baseball career by playing catch in the backyard with his mom. Steven Baez Rosario plays shortstop, outfield, and pitcher. Alan Hubbard plays catcher and pitcher. Christy Conway, who plays second base, began by playing tee-ball.

Possible Topics for Further Investigation

1 Many of the kids interviewed in *Baseball Kids* have favorite players and teams. Have a team of student interviewers gather information and make interesting bar graphs related to major league baseball. For example, have each of four students ask 25 kids in the school, "What is your favorite major league baseball team?" Interviewers should record the responses, pool their information, and graph the results for the class to see.

2 At least one of the baseball players interviewed in this book mentioned that he prefers using an aluminum bat. Ask a pair of students to research bats, with the help of the school physical education teacher or a local baseball coach. How long and how heavy is the standard bat used in the big leagues? Can aluminum bats be used at all levels? What are the differences between aluminum bats and wooden bats? Have the students share their findings with the class.

3 The traits of the coach affect not only the skill development of the players but also the attitude of the team toward their sport. These same traits apply to nonsporting events; for example, when one student coaches another in an academic skill. Have a group of students make a list of do's and don'ts for coaches. Have them ask others what traits characterize good and poor coaches and combine the comments into a short chart (no more than six do's and six don'ts). Post the chart in the classroom.

📖 *Batboy: An Inside Look at Spring Training*

by Joan Anderson
photographs by Matthew Cavanaugh
New York: Lodestar Books, 1996. 48p. (unnumbered)

This nonfiction book tells the story of Kenny Garibaldi, a batboy for the San Francisco Giants. It is used here as a bridge book because it tells Kenny's story and also gives basic, factual information. It includes many color photographs and will appeal to readers in grades three through five. It also includes a glossary of terms.

Kenny plays catcher on a Babe Ruth League baseball team. His neighbor, Kirt Manwaring, is the catcher for the San Francisco Giants. Kenny goes to spring training with his hero and get a job as a batboy because his dad is the team photographer.

Batboys work alongside players, coaches, and managers. They have a tough job and put in long hours. During spring vacation, Kenny works all day at the clubhouse. On school days, he works at night, cleaning. He says that you learn the job "by doing it."

Kenny is responsible for many specific duties. He helps to keep the game going smoothly without drawing attention to himself. For the first few hours on a game day, Kenny sorts uniforms, delivers fan mail, answers the phone, and makes endless trips to the laundry room. Before game-day practice, Kenny sets out towels and batting helmets. Just before the game begins, he sets out the rosin bag, pine tar, and towels for the batters. During the game, Kenny darts on and off the field to give the umpire more balls and to pick up helmets, masks, and bats. By the end of the game day, Kenny has put in 14 long hours.

Possible Topics for Further Investigation

1   A glossary of terms, some of which may be new to readers, is included in this book. Have three students work together using graph paper to make a baseball crossword puzzle (including clues and an answer key) that includes words from the book's glossary. Photocopy the puzzle for the class to solve.

2   The San Francisco Giants hold their spring training in Scottsdale, Arizona. Spring training sites have warm temperatures and are places where residents and tourists come and watch the games. Have a group of interested students, with the help of a media specialist, research where all the major league baseball teams hold their spring training. Have the students make a map of the United States that shows each team's spring training site with a colored dot. Students should label cities and states on the map and make a legend to identify teams by color. Have the students share the map with the class.

3   Being able to say "no" politely is a skill. In this book, Kenny explains that when fans ask him to get autographs, he must deny their requests. Invite a pair of students to role play this situation for the class. One student will play an eager fan while the other will play the batboy. Have the class comment on the conversation and how the batboy might have been more effective in dealing with the fan. Ask students to suggest a situation in which a request is denied that might occur at school. Have two students role play this situation.

From *Exploring the World of Sports.* © 1998 Phyllis J. Perry. Teacher Ideas Press. (800) 237-6124.

📖 *At the Crack of the Bat*

compiled by Lillian Morrison
illustrated by Steve Cieslawski
New York: Hyperion Books for Children, 1992. 64p.

This collection of baseball poetry will appeal to kindergarten through fifth-grade students. In addition to the poems, a section titled "Notes on Ballplayers" contains short paragraphs of biographical information on more than a dozen ballplayers. Included are full-page color illustrations and many action sketches reproduced as brown on white.

Some of the poems refer to famous teams and players. A classroom with knowledgeable and partisan fans will enjoy such poems as "The Yankees" by Robert Lord Keyes, "Nolan Ryan" by Gene Fehler, "Baseball's Sad Lexicon" by Franklin P. Adams, "Tinker to Evers?" by Steve Vittori, "Along Came Ruth" by Ford Frick, "Jackie Robinson" by Lucille Clifton, "Hammerin' Hank" by D. Roger Martin, "For Junior Gilliam" by B. H. Fairchild, and "The Great One" by Tom Clark.

Other poems are seasonal, such as "Tomorrow" by Milton Bracker, "End of Winter" by Eve Merriam, "Hail" by Scott Barry, and "October" by Hester Jewell Dawson.

Many of the poems contain elements of humor, including "Analysis of Baseball" by May Swenson, "The Abominable Baseball Bat" by X. J. Kennedy, "Donnybrook at Riverfront Stadium" by Lillian Morrison, "First Time at Third" by Jacqueline Sweeney, "The New Kid" by Mike Makley, "The Home-Watcher" by Milton Bracker, and "Bottom of the Ninth Haiku" by R. Gerry Fabian.

Discussion Starters and Multidisciplinary Activities

1   In the poem "The Abominable Baseball Bat" by X. J. Kennedy, the reader is not told exactly what happened. Discuss the poem and have students offer their interpretations.

2   Richard Armour's humorous poem "Numbers Game" appears on page 17. It may take more than one reading to fully understand this short poem. Ask students to discuss and explain which players are out and why.

3   Discuss with students the poem "The Red Stockings" on page 41. What does the poet mean about "mattress" and "cage"? Are the Red Stockings a modern team or a team that played baseball a long time ago?

4   On page 48, the poem "Wamby or The Nostalgic Record Book" by Milton Bracker describes how someone made a triple play unassisted. Have an interested student use a diagram of a baseball diamond to show how this could happen. Have another student, with the help of a media specialist, research the unassisted triple play that occurred in the 1920 World Series and tell the class about it.

5   On page 14, "Pull Hitter" by R. Gerry Fabian uses shape to help convey meaning. After discussing this shape poem, invite students to write a short poem about some aspect of baseball. Have them use line length or shape to convey meaning.

6   Some elementary school physical education classes specialize in skilled jump roping. Ask the physical education teacher to incorporate into the gym class some of the jump-rope rhymes from the book.

Nonfiction Connections

📖 *Baseball's Greatest Hitters*

📖 *Belles of the Ballpark*

📖 *Everyone Wins at Tee-Ball*

📖 *The Great American Baseball Strike*

📖 *Hank Aaron*

📖 *The Illustrated Rules of Baseball*

📖 *Jackie Robinson Breaks the Color Line*

📖 *Jose Canseco: Baseball Superstar, Famous Record Breaker*

📖 *Josh Gibson: Baseball Great*

📖 *A Kid's Guide to Collecting Baseball Cards*

📖 *Leagues Apart: The Men and Times of the Negro Baseball Leagues*

Baseball's Greatest Hitters

by S. A. Kramer
illustrated by Jim Campbell
New York: Random House, 1995. 48p.

This book, devoted to the stories of great hitters, will appeal to students in grades two through four. It is part of the Step Into Reading Books series and includes black-and-white photographs and color drawings depicting famous hitters throughout the history of baseball.

The book begins by stating that one of the hardest jobs in sports is making the right decision as a batter. The first hitter discussed is Honus Wagner, who had a long career with the Pittsburgh Pirates. He was the most powerful hitter in a period known as the Dead Ball Era. During this period, from 1897 to 1917, he won eight batting titles.

Another of the great hitters was Ty Cobb, one of baseball's most unpopular heroes. He did everything possible to make players hate him, yet he has the highest lifetime batting average of any player. He spent most of his career with the Detroit Tigers.

A chapter is devoted to the most powerful of the sluggers, Babe Ruth, whose lifetime slugging average was .690. His career with the Boston Red Sox and the New York Yankees spanned the period from 1914 to 1935.

Ted Williams played for the Boston Red Sox from 1939 to 1960; he holds the highest single-season percentage as a hitter, .551. In 1974, Hank Aaron, playing for the Atlanta Braves against the Dodgers, broke the home-run lifetime record of Babe Ruth by hitting his 715th home run. Other great hitters included are Joe Jackson, Rogers Hornsby, Lou Gehrig, Josh Gibson, Stan Musial, and Willie Mays.

Possible Topics for Further Investigation

1 Researchers in any field rely upon knowledge of specialized sources of information. Have a pair of students make an appointment with a school or city librarian to discuss sources of information available to those studying sports. Have the students take notes on special encyclopedias, vertical files, reference books, magazines, and other sources and share the information with the class. To help students learn how to use research materials, have them try to answer the following question: Hank Aaron was one of only four players in the history of baseball to achieve a lifetime record of 3,000 hits, 300 home runs, and 200 stolen bases. Who were the other three players?

2 This book explains that a baseball is only 2.868 inches wide. Ask a group of three students to work on a measuring project: How would you go about measuring an object that is round? Is there more than one way to measure it? What is the exact size in inches and in centimeters of a golf ball, a softball, a volleyball, and a soccer ball? Have the students share their findings with the class.

3 Teach math using baseball data. Invite students to clip baseball articles from the sports section of a newspaper and make up related math story problems (including an answer key). Post the problems in a special place each day for one week and have the class solve them for extra credit. All data needed to solve the problems should be included. The problems might involve ticket prices, extra base hits, runs batted in, season batting averages, amount of decrease or increase in a batting average as a result of a single game, stolen bases, or home runs.

📖 *Belles of the Ballpark*

by Diana Star Helmer
Brookfield, CT: Millbrook Press, 1993. 96p.

This book will appeal to fourth- and fifth-grade readers. It is illustrated with black-and-white photographs.

For the most part, professional baseball has been a male-dominated sport. However, there was a brief period of time, from 1943 to 1954, when more than 500 women from Cuba, Canada, and the United States earned their living playing professional baseball.

This book tells the story of these belles of the ballpark. The women's league was founded by wealthy chewing-gum magnate, Philip Wrigley, who owned the Chicago Cubs. When the United States was involved in World War II—and many men were called to active duty in the armed services—Wrigley decided that women could keep professional baseball alive.

The book explains how the women lived with local families and how they were chaperoned when they were on the road. It details their uniforms and their training, which included charm school as well as batting, catching, and throwing. In addition to the Big Belles, there were junior teams—in Racine, Kenosha, Rockford, Fort Wayne, and Muskegon—in which girls ages 12 to 14 could play.

In the 1950s, the popularity of women's and girls' baseball began to fade. By the mid-1950s, men's teams were again drawing the crowds. A special exhibit in the Cooperstown National Baseball Hall of Fame is dedicated to the women's league.

Possible Topics for Further Investigation

1 This book describes a dramatic social change that took place in the United States during World War II. Women began to work in factories and shipyards because so many men were involved in the war effort. Have a group of students, with the help of a media specialist, find materials dealing with women's war-effort work (including pictures, if possible) and research this era of U.S. history. Have the students share their findings with the class.

2 Not only did women work in factories and shipyards and play professional baseball during this era, they entered the armed services as well. Have a group of students research this era to learn what branches of armed service were opened to women during World War II, what the women's service groups were called, and what these women did during the war. Have the students prepare a written report titled "The Involvement of Women in the Armed Services During World War II" and share it with the class.

3 Long after World War II, professions that had been exclusively women's were opened to men. Instead of just female airline stewardesses, for example, there are now male flight attendants. Some fields of work are still predominately male or female. When a member of the opposite sex breaks into one of these fields, it is still considered newsworthy. Have students make a scrapbook of typical and atypical workers and professionals from a variety of fields. Magazine articles and pictures should be included. Place the career scrapbooks in the classroom library.

 ## *Everyone Wins at Tee-Ball*

**NONFICTION
CONNECTIONS**

by Henry Grosshandler and Janet Grosshandler
New York: Cobblehill Books, 1990. 32p. (unnumbered)

Because tee-ball can be played by boys and girls who are six, seven, or eight years old, this book will appeal to students in grades one through three. It is illustrated with color photographs.

This book explains that children do not need to know how to play tee-ball to join a team and work with coaches on their game. Coaches teach the children how to hold and use a bat, and the ball is placed on a hitting tee. Boys and girls try to hit the ball off the tee. If they miss, they try again.

Children learn to play all nine positions on the team and rotate throughout the season. They practice hitting, catching, throwing, running, and fielding. Score is not kept in tee-ball. Everyone wears a helmet when batting, and the catcher wears special equipment. Boys and girls wear caps and shirts in team colors.

In tee-ball, teams plays four innings. While one team is in the field, everyone on the other team gets a turn to hit the ball. After a hit, the batter runs the bases, just as one does in baseball. After everyone has had a turn at bat, the fielders come in and the batters go out into the field. During midseason, a coach will sometimes pitch to give players practice hitting a thrown ball instead of one on the tee. Toward the end of the season, a coach pitches every game.

The book concludes with a note to parents about attending games, and helping their children succeed and have fun.

Possible Topics for Further Investigation

1 Some towns and cities have little in the way of organized sports; others have much to offer. Coaches and team organizers often say that it is difficult to advertise their sporting activities so that they reach prospective players with accurate information. Have a small group of students contact various youth sporting groups which offer activities that are free and open to children in elementary school. Have students use word processing or desktop publishing software to print a one-page flyer, including such information as age requirements, registration and tryout dates and times, and telephone numbers of contacts. Emphasize the importance of proofreading and accuracy. Post the flyer on a school bulletin board or, with the permission of the sporting groups, publish it in a school newsletter.

2 In most baseball stories, much attention is given to the final score, batting averages, strikeouts, and so on. This can't happen in a story about tee-ball because a batter is up until he or she gets a hit, and an inning isn't over until each member of each team has batted successfully. Encourage a pair of students to write a sports article about an imaginary (or real) tee-ball game. What sorts of information could they include in the story?

3 Have a pair of students write and illustrate a picture book about a child's first game of tee-ball. The central character can be a boy or girl assigned to play any position on the team. Arrange a time for the students to visit a kindergarten class and read their story aloud.

 The Great American Baseball Strike

by Joe Layden
Brookfield, CT: Millbrook Press, 1995. 64p.

This book will appeal to fourth- and fifth-grade readers. It contains five chapters, is illustrated with photographs, and includes charts and graphs.

Chapter One, "Strike!" discusses the baseball strike that began in August 1994 and lasted 234 days. The strike was about money. The players refused to accept management's proposal of a salary cap and started the longest work stoppage in the history of major league baseball. Players thought that management would bargain rather than lose the lucrative television rights to the World Series. In the fall of 1994, for the first time since 1904, there was no World Series.

Chapter Two, "The American Pastime," traces the history of baseball from its beginnings in 1845 with the New York Knicker-bocker Base Ball Club. The first professional team, the Cincinnati Red Stockings, took the field in 1869.

Chapter Three, "Labor Woes," traces the formation and the development of a labor union for professional baseball players. In 1890, disputes led to a players league and a national league. Chapter Four, "Field of Dreams?" describes the actions taken after the 1994 baseball strike when President Clinton appointed a federal mediator to try to negotiate a settlement. Spring training began with replacement players.

Chapter Five, "As American as Apple Pie," discusses the importance of baseball in American culture and the many pressures brought to bear to finally end the baseball strike.

Possible Topics for Further Investigation

1 In 1885, John Montgomery formed the first union for professional baseball players. It was disbanded in 1890, and things on the labor front were quiet until 1966. Have a small group of students, with the help of a media specialist, research the status of labor unions in other fields. Was labor organized successfully in any area? Which unions were powerful? Who were their leaders? Were there famous strikes? Where did they occur and how were they settled? Have students share with the class what they learn.

2 One rich source of revenue for baseball is the televised World Series games. Ask three students who have a dramatic and humorous bent to write and present a sports commentary acting as announcers for one inning of a pretend World Series game. Have them create imaginary players and teams, fanciful nicknames, and dramatic moments, such as pitcher's duels, home runs, dropped fly balls, and so on. Have the students present a live or recorded commentary to the class.

3 Many people have argued that if the position of baseball commissioner had been filled with a powerful and competent leader during the summer of 1994, a baseball strike would never have occurred. Have a pair of students, with the help of an adult volunteer or a media specialist, research the office of baseball commissioner. What are the names of the people who have served in that capacity, and what years did they serve? Have the students display the information in chart form in the classroom.

📖 *Hank Aaron*

by James Tackach
New York: Chelsea House, 1992. 64p.

NONFICTION CONNECTIONS

This book, illustrated with black-and-white photographs, will appeal to readers in grades three through five. It is part of a series of books, Baseball Legends.

Chapter 1 describes how Hank Aaron, a veteran of 20 seasons with the Milwaukee and Atlanta Braves, broke Babe Ruth's long-standing record of home runs. On April 8, 1974, Hank Aaron broke that record when he hit his 715th home run.

The remainder of the book describes the long and remarkable career of this outstanding ballplayer. Chapter 2 tells about his Alabama boyhood while Chapter 3 describes his beginnings in professional baseball when he played for the Indianapolis Clowns in the Negro leagues. Chapter 4 tells of his banner season of 1955 with the Braves when he was selected to play in an All Star game.

Chapter 5 chronicles Hank Aaron's championship seasons with the Braves. In 1957, he hit an 11th-inning home run to win the National League Pennant for the Braves. That same year, they went on to win the World Series against the New York Yankees. The next year, the Braves and Yankees again faced each other in the World Series, but this time, the Yanks won. After that, although the Braves did poorly, Hank Aaron continued to perform well.

Chapter 6, "The Race," tells of the years in which Aaron amassed home runs until, in 1974, he surpassed Babe Ruth's record. Chapter 7 describes his final two seasons after being traded to the Milwaukee Brewers.

Possible Topics for Further Investigation

1 Have a small group of students work together to prepare a set of baseball-related math story problems for the class to solve, using data from page 61, which shows Hank Aaron's major league statistics from 1954 through 1976. Each student in the group should write out a problem, solve it, and then give it to the other group members to solve. Answers should be compared; if they do not agree, further work should be done to ensure that the problem is written clearly and that the correct answer appears in the answer key.

2 A player cannot be elected to the Baseball Hall of Fame until after retirement, but student baseball fans will surely have favorites among active players. Encourage a group of interested students to establish an "Active Players Hall of Fame." First, have them research their favorite players and gather necessary information. Students might want to write a list of achievements for each player, similar in style to the plaque shown on page 60. Post the "Active Players Hall of Fame" in the classroom.

3 Have students who enjoy doing pencil, charcoal, or pen-and-ink sketches work together to complete a series of sketches, with captions, that depict the high points of Hank Aaron's professional life. They might show him hitting the home run that broke Babe Ruth's record, leaping high in the outfield to catch a long fly ball, celebrating his team's win in the World Series, or sliding into third base. Post the sketches on a classroom bulletin board.

📖 *The Illustrated Rules of Baseball*

NONFICTION CONNECTIONS

by Dennis Healy
illustrated by Patrick T. McRae
Nashville, TN: Ideals Children's Books, 1995. 32p.

This book, which introduces young players to the basic rules of baseball, is appropriate for students in grades two through four.

Rule 1 delineates the playing field, using a diagram to show the location of the backstop, home plate, batter's boxes, coach's box, and dugouts. Rules 2 and 3 describe the size, weight, and materials of balls and bats. Rule 4 explains the three basic types of mitts or gloves used in baseball. Rule 5 describes all the other types of clothing and equipment used.

Rule 6 describes the length of the game and the use of extra innings in the event of a tie. Rules 7 and 8 show where the players on the defensive team are located when they take their positions and where the umpire, who is the main official, stands.

Rules 9, 10, and 11 deal with the batter's box, the strike zone, and strikes. Rule 12 describes pitching positions, and Rules 13 and 14 explain how a player is called out or takes a base on balls. Rule 15 clarifies fair and foul territory, Rules 16 and 17 explain hits and runs, and Rule 18 explains when a runner is safe. Rule 19 describes errors, and Rule 20 explains stolen bases.

The book concludes with a description of all the positions and required skills, an explanation of the umpire's signals, a discussion of sportsmanship, and definitions of baseball terms.

Possible Topics for Further Investigation

1   The author of this book, Dennis Healy, played major league baseball and serves as an umpire for American Legion Baseball. The job of a professional baseball umpire is difficult. Have a pair of students research this topic. How does one prepare for a career as a major league umpire? What training is necessary? Are there schools for umpires? Do umpires, like players, often begin in the minor leagues and, with skill and experience, move up into the major leagues? Have the students share with the class what they learn.

2   Page 7 of this book gives the dimensions of a baseball diamond for youth leagues and for professional leagues, explaining where and how far from one another the bases and the pitcher's mound are located. Have a pair of students make a scale drawing of each playing field, using an appropriate scale of feet to inches, which should be included in a legend. Graphing paper might be appropriate for this activity. Post the two scale drawings on a classroom bulletin board.

3   Rule 4 discusses the various gloves or mitts used by baseball players: the catcher's mitt, the first baseman's mitt, and the fielder's glove. Invite a little league coach to visit the class and bring one of each kind of mitt or glove. Ask the coach to point out the differences and explain how the shape of each mitt or glove aids the player. After the visit, have students write a thank you letter to the guest.

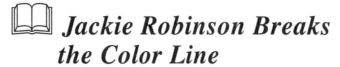 *Jackie Robinson Breaks the Color Line*

NONFICTION CONNECTIONS

by Andrew Santella
Danbury, CT: Childrens Press, 1996. 32p.

This book, illustrated with black-and-white photographs, will appeal to readers in grades three through five. It explains how Branch Rickey, general manager of the Brooklyn Dodgers in 1945, sought to defeat racism in national league baseball by signing Jackie Robinson to play for the Montreal Royals, one of the Dodger's minor league teams.

Branch Rickey had scouts looking for just the right player to break the "color line." He needed a fine baseball player—someone courageous and smart enough to deal with difficult situations. Jackie Robinson was selected for the assignment.

Robinson grew up in California and participated in every sport in high school. He attended UCLA on a scholarship and became the first student there to earn varsity letters in four sports. He left school in 1941, before graduating, to find a job and help support his mother. Within a few months, he was drafted into the army at the beginning of World War II.

After his service in the army, Robinson joined the Kansas City Monarchs in the Negro leagues. In 1945, he left the Monarchs to play on a minor league Dodgers team in Canada, the Montreal Royals. With his help, the Royals won the International League Pennant.

Though the baseball team owners voted 15 to 1 to keep Robinson out of the major leagues, the baseball commissioner, Happy Chandler, overruled the vote. Robinson made baseball history when he stepped onto the field in a Dodgers uniform in 1947. By the end of the season, he had been named the National League Rookie of the Year. Robinson won many honors and played for the Dodgers for 10 years, helping them to win six pennants.

Possible Topics for Further Investigation

1 Although Jackie Robinson was one of the first great African American ballplayers, he was followed by many others. Have pairs of students research and write reports about other great black sports figures to share with the class. Possible baseball greats include Larry Doby, Roy Campanella, Minnie Minoso, Willie Mays, Ernie Banks, Henry Aaron, and Frank Robinson. Ask students to discuss what it is about team sports that made it an area in which discrimination started to break down.

2 Jackie Robinson had difficulty with racism while he was in the army. Military police arrested him for refusing to move to the back of a bus at Fort Hood. He faced a military court-martial for disobedience, but he was found not guilty and given an honorable discharge. Have a small group of students research the system of courts-martial. What citizens are tried in a court-martial? Who serves as judge/jury? Do soldiers have an attorney to represent them as they would in a civil court? What types of punishment can courts-martial give? In an oral presentation, have the students share with the class what they learn.

3 In the 1940s, Jackie Robinson faced a court-martial for refusing to move to the back of a bus on the Fort Hood army post. Rosa Parks, in 1955, refused to give up her bus seat in Montgomery, Alabama. This led to a successful boycott of buses organized by Martin Luther King Jr. Invite a pair of interested students to research this topic. What happened after Rosa Parks refused to give up her bus seat? What was Martin Luther King Jr.'s involvement in this civil rights effort?

📖 *Jose Canseco: Baseball Superstar, Famous Record Breaker*

NONFICTION CONNECTIONS

by Bettina Ling
Austin, TX: Raintree Steck-Vaughn, 1996. 48p.

This book is part of a series, Contemporary Hispanic Americans. It will appeal to students in grades three through five.

In his first season in the major leagues, Jose Canseco was named Rookie of the Year. In his third year, he became the "40-40 man," the first player in 112 years of major league baseball to hit 40 home runs and steal 40 bases in the same year.

Jose Canseco and his twin brother were born in Havana, Cuba, in 1964. His family lived a comfortable life until Castro took control of Cuba. The Cansecos emigrated to the United States in 1965.

The two brothers played baseball as they grew up in Florida, where Jose's brother, Ozzie, had the reputation as a better ballplayer than Jose. During his senior year in high school, Jose came into his own as a hitter. He was spotted by a scout for the Oakland Athletics and signed to play for them. Ozzie was signed to play for the New York Yankees.

After playing AAA-class baseball, Jose entered the major leagues. After a great hitting year in 1988, Jose had a host of personal problems and injuries and was traded in 1992 to the Texas Rangers. In 1993, he injured his arm. After a period of therapy, Jose began to make a comeback in 1994 as a hitter for the Boston Red Sox.

Possible Topics for Further Investigation

1   The Canseco family emigrated to the United States from Cuba. To do so, they had to apply for visas. Ask a small group of students to research visas and immigration policies for the United States. How can a person enter the United States from Cuba, Mexico, Canada, Russia, Germany, England, and France? Where does one get an application for a visa? Are there quotas? How long is the average wait to receive a visa for someone from each of the above countries? Must the emigrant have relatives or a job waiting for them in the United States? Have the students share with the class what they learn.

2   The United States has had a stormy history with Cuba. Invite a small group of students to research past and present relations between the two countries. Have the students prepare a chart of specific events and dates that mark special occasions in the history of relations between the United States and Cuba. Have the students use their chart to discuss this history with the class.

3   Not far from Cuba is Puerto Rico. The history between Puerto Rico and the United States has been interesting. It has been proposed that Puerto Rico should become one of the states of the United States. Have a group of students make a list of pros and cons for adding Puerto Rico as a 51st state. Have the students share this information with the class and then take a poll of the students on whether or not to annex Puerto Rico. How would students redesign our flag to include 51 stars?

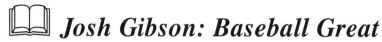 *Josh Gibson: Baseball Great*

NONFICTION CONNECTIONS

by John B. Holway

New York: Chelsea House, 1995. 112p.

This book is appropriate for students in grades four and five. It is part of the Black Americans of Achievement series and is illustrated with black-and-white photographs. The book details the events of the short life of Josh Gibson, who lived during a time when black players were not allowed in major league baseball.

After moving from Georgia to Pennsylvania, Gibson began playing for the New York Homestead Grays, one of the best baseball teams in the Negro leagues. In 1930, at age 18, Gibson played in a championship series in Yankee Stadium and hit the longest fly ball that has ever been hit at the stadium: The ball sailed 505 feet from home plate.

Josh Gibson went to the Homestead Grays's spring training in Hot Springs, Arkansas. He proved to be a remarkable catcher; developed a short, quick swing; and seldom struck out. Although he was a big man, Gibson was also a fast runner. Offered a raise in pay, he and several other Grays players left in 1932 to play for the Pittsburgh Crawfords. There, he played with another famous black player, Satchel Paige.

Eventually, the Grays enticed Gibson to return. Gibson played one of his best years in 1939, when he scored 17 home runs in 88 batting attempts. He again left the Grays in 1940, this time to play in Latin America. He returned to the Grays.

In 1943, Gibson fell into a coma and was hospitalized. After that, he was in and out of hospitals for the remainder of his life. Three months before Jackie Robinson joined the major leagues, Josh Gibson died at age 35.

Possible Topics for Further Investigation

1. Chapter 8 of this book briefly describes the attack on Pearl Harbor and the outbreak of World War II. The author mentions that Josh Gibson, then 30 years old, was not called for military service. Many students will be unfamiliar with the details of the draft that called men to serve in the armed forces during this time. Have a pair of students, with the help of a media specialist, research the draft. How was it organized? What classifications were used? What ages of men were called to serve? What conditions caused a man to be rejected? In an oral report, have the students share with the class what they learn.

2. Joe Louis is briefly mentioned on page 110 of this book. In 1946, Joe Louis knocked out the heavyweight boxing challenger, Billy Conn. Have a pair of interested students research the boxing career of Joe Louis. When did he become a boxing champion? How many times did he successfully defend his title? Who succeeded him as heavyweight champion? Have the students write a report, citing their sources, to share what they learn about this black athlete.

3. An essay by Coretta Scott King is included in this book. Have a pair of students, with the help of an adult volunteer or a media specialist, answer the following questions: Who is Coretta Scott King? What made her husband so famous? When and where did he die? What holiday commemorates his life and death? Are special events held in your town on this date? What phrase in a speech he made is especially famous?

📖 *A Kid's Guide to Collecting Baseball Cards*

NONFICTION CONNECTIONS

by Casey Childress, with Linda McKenzie
Tucson, AZ: Harbinger House, 1994. 68p.

This book will be of interest to elementary school students of all ages. Casey Childress began collecting baseball cards when he was 12. He was helped in writing this book by his mother, Linda. The book is illustrated with black-and-white cartoon drawings.

A few of the pages in this book are designed for the reader's use, including "My Personal Stats," a five-page "Baseball Cards Checklist," and two pages for notes. However, if you are using a library's copy of this book, have students use their own paper on which to make notes.

Among the topics in the book are "Why Collect Baseball Cards, Anyway?" "What You'll Need," "Help from Books and Magazines," "Organizing Your Cards," "Buying, Selling, and Trading Cards," "Which Cards to Collect," "Getting Autographs," "Other Things to Collect," "Card Shows and Conventions," "You're on Deck," "A Note to Moms and Dads," and "More Good Stuff." The section "More Good Stuff" includes information on assessing card condition and common words and terms related to collecting baseball cards.

The book is a helpful guide to the beginning baseball-card collector. It gives information on how to buy, sell, and trade cards and how to protect and organize the cards into a fine collection. Tips for collectors, enclosed in card-shaped borders, are sprinkled throughout the book. The book stresses throughout that collecting baseball cards can be a fun and rewarding hobby.

Possible Topics for Further Investigation

1. The author explains that one way to organize a collection of baseball cards is to store them in a three-ring notebook in plastic pages. Eighteen cards, nine to a side, can be stored in a notebook page. A danger, however, is that some kinds of plastic pages contain a chemical to make them flexible; the cards might absorb this chemical and begin to deteriorate. The author recommends Mylar pages. Have a student research plastic pages. What chemical is used to keep them flexible? What is Mylar and how is it different in manufacture? In an oral report, have the student share this information with the class.

2. This book includes a list of magazines that might be of interest to baseball-card collectors. Have a pair of students look for copies of available magazines at the school or city library and bring them to class to share. Among those mentioned are *Beckett's Baseball Card Monthly*, *Baseball Cards*, *Baseball Card News*, *Sports Collectors Digest*, *Street & Smith's Baseball*, *Sports Illustrated*, and *Sports Illustrated for Kids*.

3. Using graph paper, have a pair of students make a baseball-related crossword puzzle (including an answer key). They might include names of players, positions, and equipment, or even words and terms related to collecting baseball cards (from the section "More Good Stuff"). Have students check their clues or definitions for accuracy. Photocopy the puzzle for the class to solve.

From *Exploring the World of Sports*. © 1998 Phyllis J. Perry. Teacher Ideas Press. (800) 237-6124.

📖 *Leagues Apart:*
The Men and Times of
the Negro Baseball Leagues

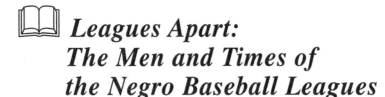

by Lawrence S. Ritter
illustrated by Richard Merkin
New York: Morrow Junior Books, 1995. 40p. (unnumbered)

Students in grades two through four will enjoy this large-format book. The illustrations are brightly colored. The text explains the men and times of the Negro baseball leagues.

Many fine black ballplayers began their careers in the Negro leagues. Before 1950, black baseball players who wanted to earn a living playing baseball played for one of the Negro league baseball teams.

Smokey Joe Williams, a pitcher with a remarkable fast ball, played for the Chicago American Giants, the New York Lincoln Giants, and the Homestead Grays. Another black pitcher for the New York Lincoln Giants was Cannonball Dick Redding. James "Cool Papa" Bell, a swift outfielder, played in the Negro baseball leagues from the early 1920s into the 1940s.

Readers learn what it was like prior to the passage of civil rights laws in the 1960s. Black ballplayers often found that hotels would not let them have a room, and that restaurants would not serve them meals.

Leroy "Satchel" Paige, a pitcher, was 42 years old by the time racial segregation, which had prevented him from playing ball in the major leagues, broke down. He signed with the Cleveland Indians in 1948, only one year after Jackie Robinson became the first black player in the major leagues. Other teams began signing black players, and the Negro leagues were soon disbanded.

Possible Topics for Further Investigation

1   Have a small group of students research the civil rights legislation of the 1960s. What kinds of laws were passed? What effect did these laws have? Who was president of the United States at the time? Which senators and congressmen led the fight for civil rights? How were these laws received in various parts of the country? In a panel discussion, have the students share this information with the class.

2   Students might be surprised to learn that for many years in movies and on television, even after televisions were common in households, blacks played only the roles of servants. Have a small group of students, with the help of a media specialist, research how film and television gradually broadened the opportunities for black actors. Have the students share with the class what they learn and point out which current movies and television series feature black actors and actresses in major roles.

3   Though Jackie Robinson was chosen as the first black player to enter major league baseball, many black players possessed the traits that would have allowed them to succeed in this role. Hold a class discussion in which students identify what traits they would look for in choosing a player to break the "color line." Why would these traits be needed for this difficult role? Encourage a few students to research Jackie Robinson and then share with the class whether they think he possessed these traits.

Part II
Basketball

Basketball

● FICTION ●

- 📖 *Benched!*
- 📖 *Choosing Sides*
- 📖 *Crane's Rebound*
- 📖 *Go to the Hoop!*
- 📖 *My Brother the Star*
- 📖 *Nutty Can't Miss*

- 📖 *On the Line*
- 📖 *Point Guard*
- 📖 *Red-Hot Hightops*
- 📖 *The Revenge of Ho-Tai*
- 📖 *Sara Kate: Superkid*

◆ BRIDGES AND POETRY ◆

- 📖 *Dave Bing: Basketball Great with a Heart*
- 📖 *Magic Johnson: Hero on and off the Court*
- 📖 *The Break Dance Kids: Poems of Sport, Motion, and Locomotion*

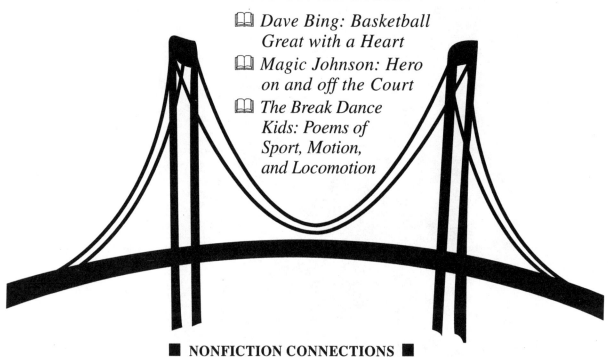

■ NONFICTION CONNECTIONS ■

- 📖 *Basketball's Greatest Players: The Year in Sports 1994*
- 📖 *Chicago Bulls*
- 📖 *Houston Rockets, Basketball Champions: The Year in Sports 1994*
- 📖 *Kareem Abdul-Jabbar*
- 📖 *Larry Bird*

- 📖 *Michael Jordan: Basketball to Baseball and Back*
- 📖 *Shaquille O'Neal*
- 📖 *Sports Great Dominique Wilkins*
- 📖 *The Story of Basketball*
- 📖 *Wilt Chamberlain*
- 📖 *The Young Basketball Player*

—OTHER TOPICS TO EXPLORE—

—3-point shots	—draft	—NBA	—referees
—basketball camps	—dribbling	—NCAA	—special shoes
—divisions	—endorsements	—playoffs	—types of fouls

From *Exploring the World of Sports.* © 1998 Phyllis J. Perry. Teacher Ideas Press. (800) 237-6124.

● *Fiction* ●

📖 *Benched!*

📖 *Choosing Sides*

📖 *Crane's Rebound*

📖 *Go to the Hoop!*

📖 *My Brother the Star*

📖 *Nutty Can't Miss*

📖 *On the Line*

📖 *Point Guard*

📖 *Red-Hot Hightops*

📖 *The Revenge of Ho-Tai*

📖 *Sara Kate: Superkid*

 *Benched!*

by David Halecroft
New York: Puffin Books, 1992. 114p.

FICTION

This book is a part of the Alden All Stars series. It is easy to read and will appeal to third- through fifth-grade readers. There are no illustrations.

The central character is Woody Franklin, who eats, sleeps, and breathes basketball. Every possible moment, he is shooting hoops. At this year's tryouts for the team, everyone is surprised by Bannister. Bannister is a well-liked classmate who has a good sense of humor but is overweight. To everyone's surprise, Bannister has gone on a diet and lost most of his excess weight.

Woody and Bannister make the team and practice together shooting baskets. Woody's parents and his friends try to warn Woody that if he continues to ignore his Spanish homework, and if he doesn't come up with a good science project, he may find himself ineligible to play ball. Woody does not heed these warnings, and after doing badly on a Spanish test, he is benched.

Woody is angry that he can't play. Bannister gets anxious and begins eating a lot of junk food. The Alden school team barely wins the game that Woody sits out, and after the game, Bannister is eating everything in sight. Again Woody doesn't study his Spanish, fails the next test, and makes his friends angry.

Woody finally takes responsibility. He studies his Spanish, helps Bannister come up with a great volcano experiment for science, takes the junk food away from Bannister, and becomes eligible to play. Woody and Bannister play in the championship game, and the Alden team wins.

Discussion Starters and Multidisciplinary Activities

1   Breaking a bad habit, such as overeating or eating junk food, is hard to do. It is harder when well-meaning relatives undermine the effort, such as when Bannister's grandmother sneaks cookies into his lunch bag. Have students discuss a time when they tried to break themselves of a habit. How were they helped or hindered?

2   Woody's parents could have made him study at the kitchen table, where they would have been able to watch him and make sure that he was studying his Spanish book instead of reading a *Sports Illustrated* magazine. They didn't do this; they let Woody have full responsibility for his study habits. Have students discuss whether they think this was wise or unwise.

3   Ask students which character they most liked, Woody or Bannister. Why?

4   Ask a player or coach of a local basketball team to come to class and talk about eligibility to play on the team. Is a certain grade average required? What happens if a player is failing one class? How often is eligibility determined? Have student follow up the visit with a thank you letter to the guest.

5   Ask a small group of students to prepare a dozen math story problems for their classmates to solve. The numerical data for each of the problems should come from facts gathered from a local newspaper's sports section. Have students check the solutions and prepare an answer key. Photocopy the story problems for the class.

6   Except for the cover, there are no illustrations for *Benched!* Ask interested students to make pencil or pen-and-ink line drawings that would be appropriate for the book. Students should note the page where the illustration would appear. Post the drawings in the classroom.

📖 *Choosing Sides*

by Ilene Cooper
New York: Morrow Junior Books, 1990. 218p.

● **FICTION**

Fourth- and fifth-grade readers will enjoy this book featuring a sixth-grade boy, Jonathan Rossi. It is part of a series of books, The Kids from Kennedy Middle School. There are no illustrations.

Jonathan tries out for the basketball team because his father is enthusiastic about sports and his older brother is a quarterback. Jonathan hopes that basketball may prove to be his game. Jonathan is also becoming aware of liking a sixth-grade girl, Robin Miller. After the coach falls and injures his leg, a new coach arrives, and basketball is less fun. Days are filled with hard drills and constant ridicule for not performing well enough. Jonathan would rather be with his friends, learn to dance, and even visit with a cousin who prefers music to sports.

A new student transfers to Kennedy Middle School and joins the team. He takes Jonathan's place as center and Jonathan moves to forward. One of Jonathan's friends quits the team. Jonathan skips a couple of practices and lies about it. The Kennedy Middle School team, after losing its first two games, finally wins a game, thanks mainly to the new student. Jonathan does well in the game, but his heart is not in it.

Jonathan wants to have time to do what he likes. He'd rather go to San Francisco to a concert with his cousin than attend another sports event. He wants to quit basketball but doesn't want to disappoint his father. Jonathan writes about his dilemma for a school assignment and gives the paper to his father to read. Afterwards, with his father's knowledge, Jonathan makes the decision to quit and feels relieved that he no longer has to play basketball.

Discussion Starters and Multidisciplinary Activities

1. Ask students if they have ever been part of an activity that they really wanted to quit but hesitated to do so because it would disappoint someone. Have students discuss their situations and their solutions to these dilemmas.

2. David learned to dance from his mother. Jonathan learned from Robin. Have students discuss who taught them how to dance, or who they think they might ask to help them learn to dance.

3. Ask students to discuss whether they think Mrs. Rossi will go to the Bears-Vikings game. Have them support their opinions with information from the book.

4. This book has no illustrations. Have interested students make illustrations for the book. They should note the page in the book where the illustrations would appear. Let students use any medium they prefer.

5. Jonathan has a hard time finding the perfect greeting card for the coach who broke his leg. Invite students to make a greeting card with an appropriate verse and design. The card might be for a different occasion but should be personalized and specific.

6. Invite students who have read *Choosing Sides* to write a chapter to describe the two trips that have been planned at the end of the story: Mr. Rossi and David will drive to Minnesota to see the Bears-Vikings game; Jon will fly to San Francisco to visit Mark, hear the symphony orchestra, and see the sights. Mrs. Rossi might go either way. Have students read aloud their chapters to others in the class who have read the book.

Crane's Rebound

by Alison Jackson
illustrated by Diane Dawson Hearn
New York: Dutton Children's Books, 1991. 122p.

This book will appeal to fourth- and fifth-grade readers. The central character, Leslie Crane, will enter middle school in the fall. It is a sequel to *My Brother the Star* (see p. 38).

Leslie has just finished fifth grade and is looking forward with a mixture of dread and delight to attending two weeks of basketball camp. Leslie wishes that his best friend, Mike, had been selected to go to camp with him instead of a girl named Bobby.

At camp, Leslie rooms with Bobby's older brother and another boy named Jake. Jake is a good player but leads the others into a lot of situations in which they end up playing mean tricks on others, including Charlotte, one of Bobby's friends.

Leslie is not doing well on the court. After angering Charlotte and Bobby while following through on one of Jake's bad ideas, he tries to avoid them in the cafeteria. Leslie begins to wish that he were at home. Leslie has a little brother, Cameron, who calls him almost every night, wanting something from his big brother.

After Jake puts Leslie in another embarrassing situation with Charlotte, Leslie gets mad and fights Jake, giving him a bloody nose. Jake moves into another room. On the court, Jake misses an easy shot, and Leslie takes the ball away from him and makes a shot himself. By the end of camp, Leslie has proven himself on the court, managed to apologize to Charlotte and Bobby, and has even forgiven his little brother for demolishing his bike.

Discussion Starters and Multidisciplinary Activities

1. Making an apology is difficult; it isn't easy to find the right words. Leslie tries several times to apologize to Charlotte but doesn't go through with it. Invite students to role play Leslie's apology to Charlotte.

2. Characters in the story attend a special sports camp for two weeks. Provide time for students to share experiences they have had while away from home. Where did they go? How long did they stay? What did they do to avoid being homesick?

3. Have the class discuss Charlotte. Why do they think she thumped Leslie so hard on the back and called him "kid"? Why was she so angry after the movie? Why did she invite Leslie to dance? Was she a good friend to Bobby?

4. Because Leslie's last name is Crane, some people gave him the nickname Ichabod. Many sports heroes have nicknames. Ask a pair of students to research important sports figures and make a list of their full names and nicknames.

5. Leslie complained about the food at camp. Most cafeterias publish a menu and follow strict food-group guidelines to decide what foods will be offered each day. Invite a cafeteria manager to visit the class, discuss the food groups, and use the school menu to show how the guidelines are followed. Have students follow up with a thank you note to the guest.

6. Is there a sports camp in your area? What is its name? Who is allowed to attend? Where do students live during the camp? Have the students research and share with the class what they learn.

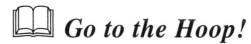 *Go to the Hoop!*

FICTION

by Dean Hughes
illustrated by Dennis Lyall
New York: Alfred A. Knopf, 1993. 104p.

This book, part of the Angel Park Hoop Stars series, will appeal to students in grades three through five. It contains black-and-white illustrations.

Harlan Sloan, a fifth-grader, is one of the youngest players on the Angel Park Lakers team. Harlan is tall and plays center, but he is a timid player. He does not leap high enough to get the tips. He passes off, almost never shoots, and is not aggressive enough at rebounding.

Coach Donaldson is always pressuring Harlan to become more aggressive, but the pressure seems to make things worse. His teammates, both boys and girls, encourage him, and so do his parents, but Harlan simply lacks the right attitude to be a winning player.

Miles, one of the best players on the Lakers team, suggests getting together with Harlan and shooting hoops. He explains to Harlan that he has to be "bad"—put on an aggressive, cocky look and attitude that will show other players that he is a force to be reckoned with.

Harlan adopts this new attitude and it serves him well. Although he still lacks confidence some of the time, he gradually is able to force himself to guard closely, draw fouls, and shoot when he is open. He also shuts out the crowd noise and succeeds from the free-throw line. After their last game, Harlan says that he's the "baddest" player on the team.

Discussion Starters and Multidisciplinary Activities

1 There are many situations in which students feel shy and lack confidence, and there are many ways to overcome such feelings. Invite students to share ways in which they have helped themselves feel more self-confident.

2 Miles was a team player. Although he was a great individual scorer, he tried hard to help the other players on the team succeed, too. Have students point out and discuss passages from the book that support this opinion of Miles.

3 Jackie Willis is one of the girls on the team; she is also one of the team leaders. Have students point out and discuss passages from the book that show Jackie's leadership on the court.

4 Have two students talk with a basketball coach and study the material on pages 94 and 95. Then have them draw a diagram on the chalkboard and explain to the class what a shuffle is and how it is used on the court.

5 Using some of the words from pages 100–104, have two students prepare a basketball crossword puzzle for classmates to solve. Have them include clues or definitions as well as an answer key. Photocopy the puzzle for the class.

6 Many of the centers that Harlan plays against have nicknames, such as Knees and House. Have a group of students who have read *Go to the Hoop!* suggest nicknames for Harlan and then vote to choose one nickname. Have these students write a chapter for the book about how Harlan got his nickname.

 # *My Brother the Star*

by Alison Jackson
illustrated by Diane Dawson Hearn
New York: E. P. Dutton, 1990. 105p.

Third- and fourth-graders will enjoy reading this novel, which is illustrated with a few humorous black-and-white illustrations. The sequel to this book is *Crane's Rebound* (see p. 36).

The central character is a tall, skinny, fifth-grade boy named Leslie Crane, sometimes called by the nickname Ichabod. Leslie is unhappy with his name and with the fact that he has a little brother, Cameron, who is always in the limelight. During the past year, Cameron has starred in several television commercials.

Leslie and his best friend, Mike, are selected to try out to represent their school at basketball camp. Cameron breaks his arm and must take a temporary hiatus from commercials. On the day of tryouts, Leslie is worried, but he does well and survives the first cut. Bobby, a fifth-grade girl, is also selected for the next round of elimination. Mike, however, is not selected.

Mike teases Leslie about the possibility of going to camp with a cute girl, Bobby. Events at home continue to go awry. The hamster escapes and can't be found. Leslie and then Cameron come down with chicken pox, so Leslie can't practice.

Mom is miserable when she learns that Cameron has grown too big for commercials and is uncooperative in the filming. Then Cameron shares with her how much he hates making commercials.

Leslie and Bobby make the final cut, are selected to go to basketball camp, and are featured in a television segment; the lost hamster is found; and everyone gathers to celebrate over pizza.

Discussion Starters and Multidisciplinary Activities

1   Leslie Crane is unhappy with his name. His mother named him after a movie star. Allow time for students who wish to do so to explain how and why their names were chosen.

2   Many of the things that Mike does in this story show that he is a good friend. Have students point out and discuss passages from the book that demonstrate this.

3   Although Cameron is a pest, he admires his brother. Have students point out and discuss passages from the book that show how Cameron truly feels about Leslie.

4   Have two students who know how to use a video camera plan and film a short news segment about the school. They may want to interview the principal, get a comment from the custodian about some event, feature a student who has won an honor, record parts of a practice session or game of one of the athletic teams, and so on. Have students share their video with the class.

5   Bobby is always blowing bubbles. Have a group of students explore soap bubbles. They can make a bubble solution using 1 cup liquid dishwashing detergent, 8 cups cold water, and 3 tablespoons glycerin; they can make bubbles using straws or wands. Why do bubbles burst? How can you touch a bubble without breaking it? How can you blow a bubble inside another bubble? Can you blow bubbles that are not round?

6   Invite students to bring to class empty cereal boxes. Have each student write a television jingle that features one of the cereals. Have students discuss which jingles are most effective.

📖 *Nutty Can't Miss*

FICTION

by Dean Hughes
New York: Atheneum, 1987. 130p.

This book, which features a fifth-grade boy and his friends, will appeal to third- through fifth-grade readers. There are no photographs or illustrations.

Freddie Nutsell, called Nutty, is uneasy at the first basketball practice because his dad is coaching the team this year in the city recreation league. When they get off to a poor start the first day—it is obvious that Mr. Nutsell knows nothing about basketball plays—Nutty goes to consult with his brainy friend, William Bilks. William agrees to be the assistant coach.

William learns some plays and teaches them, but in the first game they prove to be ineffective. The team loses, 69–13. William decides that perhaps the solution is "imaging"—seeing oneself in the act of shooting perfectly.

At first, Nutty doesn't believe that William can do anything for him. After a while, though, he begins to see the connection between his mind, the ball, and the net. In their next game, Nutty scores 41 points. He likes the feel of being a hero, especially in front of Sarah, a girl he likes.

In the games that follow, Nutty is in a trance and can't miss. His team wins easily. Nutty is uncomfortable, though. He doesn't feel emotion. In the championship game, Nutty's dad tells him to be himself. Nutty gets excited; makes the final, winning shot; and feels the emotion he's been missing.

Discussion Starters and Multidisciplinary Activities

1 Sometimes having a parent who is the student's coach, Scouts leader, or PTO president can make the student feel uncomfortable. Encourage students to discuss their feelings and thoughts about such a situation.

2 Orlando and Nutty have a complex relationship. Sometimes they are friends; sometimes they are rivals. Have students discuss this. Do they think Orlando and Nutty will be better friends after the championship game? Why?

3 Ask students to discuss whether they think William was or was not a good assistant coach. Why?

4 Imaging plays a role in many sports. Ask an interested student to locate a library book or article in which imaging is recommended to improve an athlete's performance. Have the student share this information with the class in an oral report.

5 Nutty's basketball team wears brown uniforms because they were on sale. Most basketball teams use bright colors. Encourage a pair of students to conduct a survey of uniform colors for high school, college, or professional basketball teams; graph their results; and share the graph with the class.

6 Nutty is distracted by the noise of the fans. Have a few students explore the sense of hearing and share with the class what they learn. For example, if you are blindfolded, can you identify by sound an object (coin, ruler, aluminum foil, etc.) that is dropped on the floor? Can you determine from what direction a sound comes? Can you determine the direction if one ear is covered?

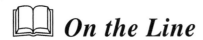 *On the Line*

FICTION

by Dean Hughes
illustrated by Dennis Lyall
New York: Alfred A. Knopf, 1993. 106p.

This book, part of the Angel Park Hoop Stars series, will appeal to readers in grades three through five. It is a sequel to *Go to the Hoop!* (see p. 37) and contains a few black-and-white illustrations.

Miles "Tip" Harris is the leading scorer for the Angel Park Lakers basketball team. The Lakers have played a good season and have a chance to play for the championship. Miles and the Lakers point guard, a girl named Jackie Willis, are black. Miles believes that some people, including his coach, are prejudiced against black players.

In an important game, Miles loses his cool when an opposing player keeps needling him with comments. Miles gets angry. He tries hard not to say anything in return but finally yells at the bench. Coach Donaldson takes Miles out of the game and is his usual grouchy self. Miles feels like the coach is picking on him, and he thinks that the coach was too hesitant in putting Jackie on the starting team.

In the games that follow, Miles tries to get control of his temper and to play his best, offensively and defensively. One day, some of the players are over at Miles's house. They are surprised when Coach Donaldson comes walking out of the house. The coach and team members speak frankly about feelings of prejudice and feel better about one another afterwards.

The Lakers go into the championship game against the Bulls. This time, Miles doesn't let the opponents distract him. He doesn't choke, and the Lakers win the game and the championship title.

Discussion Starters and Multidisciplinary Activities

1 Four types of discrimination are discussed in the book: discrimination against females, Latinos, blacks, and the poor. Have students discuss these types of discrimination and how they might help end such discrimination.

2 Miles and Coach Donaldson both changed. Have students discuss how these major characters were different at the end of the book from the way they were in the beginning.

3 Although Miles's father wanted Miles to take responsibility for his life, Miles's father said and did several things in the course of the story to try to help his son. Have students discuss what Miles's father said and did.

4 Page 99 contains a "Smart Passing Checklist." Ask students to make a colorful poster to illustrate one section of the list ("Before Passing," "When Passing," or "When Catching a Pass"). Students may use whatever medium they prefer. With permission, hang the poster in the school gymnasium.

5 First, ask two students to research the dimensions of a standard basketball court. Then have these two students watch a televised professional basketball game together and, using a notepad and pencil, trace for two minutes the path one player travels on the court. Have the students determine a scale for the diagram, based on the dimensions of a standard court, and estimate about how many feet the player traveled in two minutes.

6 First, have students research the game time for a basketball game. Then, have students use the data from activity 5 (above) to estimate how many miles a basketball player travels during the course of a game, assuming that the player plays for the entire game. Have students share their findings with the class.

FICTION

 *Point Guard*

by Dean Hughes
illustrated by Dennis Lyall
New York: Alfred A. Knopf, 1992. 102p.

This book, part of the Angel Park Hoop Stars series, will appeal to third- through fifth-grade readers. It is a sequel to *Go to the Hoop!* (see p. 37). One outstanding black-and-white drawing is included in each chapter. Both boys and girls are featured as players.

Jackie Willis is one of two girls to make the Angel Park Lakers basketball team. She plays point guard on the second string. The starting player is Tommy Ramirez. The coach is always yelling at Tommy to play harder. The coach finally sends in Jackie to play just before the end of the first half. She does a fine job, but in the second half, the coach again sends in Tommy. Most of the players recognize that Jackie is the better player and they wonder why the coach doesn't make her a starter.

The best player on the team, Miles, tries to make suggestions to the coach, including that Jackie should play, and his ideas are belittled. Some of the players wonder if the coach isn't playing Jackie because she's black or because she's a girl.

In every game, Jackie spends a lot of time on the bench. When she does play, Jackie demonstrates that she is a better player than Tommy. Finally, she meets with the coach and suggests that she "challenge" Tommy for the starting position. The coach reluctantly agrees. Jackie shows how good she is, and the coach puts her on the starting team. Under her leadership, the team wins. The coach congratulates Jackie, admits that he was wrong and old-fashioned in his prejudice against girls, and promises to work with her.

Discussion Starters and Multidisciplinary Activities

1. When Jackie proved she was a better player than Tommy, Tommy could have reacted in several ways. Have students discuss how Tommy did react to Jackie's skills.

2. Miles says that he misses his old neighborhood. Jackie's mother says that she understands, because she grew up in a black neighborhood, too. Still, she adds, they have fought for integration, and now they have to go out and take a chance. Have students discuss this conversation between Miles and Mrs. Willis.

3. Jackie convinced her father and the other players to let her approach the coach herself. Have students discuss what they think the coach would have done if the players had refused to play or if Jackie's father had complained to him.

4. Have a few interested students obtain permission from the teachers of several grades to conduct an investigation: In fifth grade, are girls and boys equal in height, or is one sex generally taller than the other? How do boys and girls in a ninth-grade class compare? Have the students make a chart to share what they learn with the class.

5. The illustrations in this book are striking. Encourage interested students to draw pencil, pen-and-ink, or charcoal illustrations to add to the book. Students should note the page in the book where the illustrations would appear. Display the illustrations in the classroom.

6. Have a pair of students survey what sports teams, if any, in your town or city commingle boys and girls or men and women on the teams. In an oral report, have the students share with the class what they learn.

📖 *Red-Hot Hightops*

FICTION

by Matt Christopher
illustrated by Paul D. Mock
Boston: Little, Brown, 1987. 148p.

This book will appeal to third- through fifth-grade readers. The central character, Kelly, plays on a middle school girls' basketball team.

The Eagles are not playing well this season. Kelly thinks that she is part of the problem. Although she plays and shoots well at practice, she seems to freeze on the court during a game. She is shy and lacks an aggressive spirit.

One day, Kelly finds a brand-new pair of red hightop shoes in her locker. They are the right size, and the coach says that it's okay to wear them, so Kelly plays a game in the shoes. Her style of play seems to change. She finds herself in the middle of key plays, and the Eagles win a game.

Kelly begins worrying about the shoes. Do they have some sort of magical power? Do they really affect how she plays on the court? Who could have put them in her locker? Does this have anything to do with two attractive boys, Anthony and Brett, who admire Kelly's playing? Or could the shoes have been planted by a fellow team member or by the odd new girl in town, Sandi?

Kelly struggles in her relationships with old and new friends and with the mystery surrounding the seemingly magical powers of the red-hot hightops. It is only after she gathers her courage and destroys the hightops that she finally discovers who gave them to her and why.

Discussion Starters and Multidisciplinary Activities

1   Sandi is an unusual character—she seems to have the ability to charm people. Kelly and the coach seem suspicious of her. Have students discuss why they think Sandi has a special effect on people.

2   Kelly's best friend is Ester. Have students discuss whether Ester is a good friend to Kelly. Why? Ask students to cite specific instances from the story to support their opinions.

3   The explanation of the magical powers of the red-hot hightops is brief. Ask students to discuss whether or not they were satisfied with the explanation. Why?

4   Many shoe stores today carry shoes for a variety of sports, including basketball, running, cross-training, walking, and so on. Invite a shoe salesperson to visit the class and bring a representative selection of athletic shoes. Ask the salesperson to point out the differences among the various kinds of shoes. Have students follow up the visit with a thank you letter to the guest.

5   The red hightops caught the attention of the crowd. Ask interested students to pretend to be sports reporters for a local newspaper and write an article about the last basketball game of the book, mentioning the red hightops. Post the articles in the classroom.

6   The illustration opposite page 116 in the book doesn't correspond with the text. Have interested students decide what the illustration should have shown and supply a new picture. Share the illustrations with the class.

📖 *The Revenge of Ho-Tai*

by Thomas Hoobler
New York: Walker, 1989. 203p.

FICTION

This book will appeal to fifth-grade readers. It is set in the present time and is told from the viewpoint of an eighth-grade boy, Roger, who attends Edwards Academy.

Edwards Academy is a small, private school and doesn't have a great basketball team. This year, the coach has taken a hiatus; the science teacher, Mr. Kapur, is coaching. From the beginning, things are different. Mr. Kapur has the boys sit on the floor and imagine themselves playing a great game.

At another practice, Mr. Kapur brings in a plaster statue that looks like the Buddha and calls it Ho-Tai. Ho-Tai becomes the team mascot, and the boys rub its belly before taking to the court. Surprisingly enough, the team members, with the exception of a bully named Dennis, improve greatly.

The girls form a cheering section. Roger's neighbor, Gabby, is one of the cheerleaders. Roger finds that he likes being around Gabby and having her as a "girlfriend" of sorts. In exchange for their cheers at basketball, the girls expect the boys to come cheer at their volleyball games.

Led by Dennis's father, parents object to Ho-Tai and to Mr. Kapur. Learning that Dennis's father will take over as coach, the eighth-graders refuse to play. Roger is expelled for fighting. A snowstorm collapses the roof of the gymnasium, built by Dennis's father, and Roger thinks that Ho-Tai has taken revenge. Roger leaves Edwards Academy for another school, taking a piece of Ho-Tai with him.

Discussion Starters and Multidisciplinary Activities

1. Although Bobby could not play on the team, he was a significant character in the book. Ask students to discuss what Bobby contributed to the story.

2. Because Roger did not start the fight with Dennis, he thought that he should not have been expelled from school. Have students discuss whether his expulsion was just.

3. Have students discuss whether they think Roger's parents had been planning all along to send Roger to a private boarding school, or whether his involvement with Ho-Tai caused them to devise this plan.

4. Roger takes a school key to a shop and has a duplicate made. Some keys are stamped "do not duplicate." Ask a pair of students to bring to class a variety of keys and explain why they are shaped as they are and what sorts of items they unlock. (The school custodian might be a good source for special keys.)

5. The roof of the gymnasium collapsed because it had not been designed with sufficient support. Ask an architect to visit the class and explain what sort of supports are necessary for a simple, rectangular gym. Ask the architect to explain architectural terms from the book, such as *crenelated wall* and *embrasure*. Have students follow up the visit with a thank you letter to the guest.

6. Invite students to pretend to be reporters for a local newspaper and write an article describing the collapse of the gymnasium at Edwards Academy. What style and tone of writing will they use? Will they mention the principal's assembly and the destruction of Ho-Tai, or will the piece be a strictly factual account? Will they quote Roger's dad or Mr. Orlotte?

📖 *Sara Kate: Superkid*

FICTION

by Susan Beth Pfeffer
illustrated by Suzanne Hankins
New York: Henry Holt, 1994. 58p.

This book will appeal to students in kindergarten through grade three. It contains humorous black-and-white illustrations.

Eight-year-old Sara Kate and her older brother, Stevie, are being watched by their grandmother while their parents are away. Stevie takes Sara Kate with him when he goes to Thompkins store to register for the basketball-throwing contest. The prize is $1,000. Sara Kate feels a strange, tingling feeling in her arm. Stevie is assigned number 42. He tells Sara Kate that if he wins, he will buy her an enormous teddy bear that she has been admiring. He'll buy himself a video game and will give his parents the rest of the money to put toward his college fund.

Back at home, Sara Kate shoots the basketball and finds that she can't miss, even from across the street. Her grandmother explains that Sara Kate has magical powers that come to some females in their family who are born on a Tuesday or a Thursday. The powers come and go and are unpredictable—they work only for a short time on Tuesdays, Thursdays, and, occasionally, Saturdays.

Sara's grandmother takes her to register for the basketball throw. During the actual contest, because Sara Kate feels her magical powers fading, she switches places with her brother so that she can shoot earlier. Her shooting amazes the crowd, but she is disqualified from winning the grand prize because she shot out of turn. Instead of the $1,000 prize, she is given a $100 gift certificate, with which she buys the teddy bear she wants and the video game for her brother.

Discussion Starters and Multidisciplinary Activities

1. Sara Kate's parents think that her grandmother tells fanciful stories, which shouldn't be taken seriously. Have students discuss whether they think Sara Kate believes her grandmother's stories about magical powers.

2. Have students discuss whether it was fair that Thompkins disqualified Sara Kate from winning the grand prize but awarded her a lesser prize instead.

3. Have students discuss Stevie's change in attitude. He was willing to help Sara Kate learn to become a good basketball player when she couldn't hit the basket, but he became angry at her and thought that she was cheating when she couldn't miss.

4. In a professional basketball game, a player scores 3 points rather than 2 points for the team if a shot is made from a certain distance from the basket. Have a pair of students research this and explain to the class from what areas of the court a player can shoot to score a 3-point basket.

5. For publicity, stores often sponsor contests involving making posters or writing essays or slogans. If a local store is sponsoring such a contest that is appropriate for the grade level of the students, secure information and help those who are interested enter the contest.

6. Stevie explained that you couldn't buy a new car with $1,000 but you might find a used car. Have students look in a local newspaper's classified ads and research how many and what kinds of cars are for sale for $1,000 or less. Have students cut out the ads and share them with the class.

From *Exploring the World of Sports*. © 1998 Phyllis J. Perry. Teacher Ideas Press. (800) 237-6124.

◆ *Bridges and Poetry* ◆

 Dave Bing: Basketball Great with a Heart

 Magic Johnson: Hero on and off the Court

 The Break Dance Kids: Poems of Sport, Motion, and Locomotion

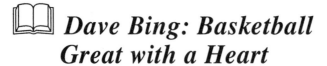 *Dave Bing: Basketball Great with a Heart*

BRIDGES AND POETRY

by Elizabeth Schleichert
Springfield, NJ: Enslow, 1995. 104p.

This book, part of the Multicultural Junior Biographies series, will appeal to fourth and fifth graders. It is divided into seven chapters, which are illustrated with black-and-white photographs. This biography serves as a bridge book because it includes factual information, and contains many quotations, woven into the text like dialogue in a story.

The book begins with the basketball game in 1966 that brought Dave Bing national attention as a new player for the Detroit Pistons. Other chapters in the book trace Dave Bing's early life as he grew up in a poor neighborhood in Washington, D.C. He showed natural athletic talent as a child. At age 12, he began playing basketball, even though he was shorter than many of the boys his age.

In high school, Dave Bing was captain of his school basketball team, as well as class treasurer. He showed the same ability as an athlete and a campus leader when he attended Syracuse University.

Bing played basketball in the National Basketball Association (NBA) for 12 years. He is one of only four players in NBA history who have been in the top 20 in both scoring and assists.

After his basketball career, he founded two companies, Bing Steel in 1980 and Superb Manufacturing in 1985. Eighty percent of his employees are African Americans. When the Detroit schools did not have enough money to fund sports, Dave Bing raised money from local businesses. His companies continue to do well, and Dave Bing is active in such organizations as Boy Scouts and Junior Achievement.

Possible Topics for Further Investigation

1 Dave Bing was invited to Washington, D.C., in 1984 to receive the National Minority Small Business Person of the Year award from President Ronald Reagan. Have a group of students, with the help of a media specialist, investigate what types of business awards are given today for minorities. Are local, state, regional, or national awards given? If so, what are these awards and who has received them? Have students share with the class what they learn.

2 When Dave Bing played basketball in the NBA, he made about $15,000 per year. Have a group of students research the annual salaries of current basketball stars. The students might want to share their information in a graph, listing salaries along the vertical axis and names of players along the horizontal axis. Have another group of students research the same for current football stars. Who are the most highly paid athletes?

3 Most sports have a Hall of Fame. Dave Bing was inducted into the Basketball Hall of Fame in 1990. Have a group of students research the Basketball Hall of Fame. How often are players inducted? Who determines which players will be added? In the most recent induction into the Basketball Hall of Fame, what were the names of the players who received this distinction? Are special ceremonies held to celebrate the induction? Where are the ceremonies held? Recruit a media specialist to help students with their investigation, and have them share with the class what they learn.

📖 *Magic Johnson: Hero on and off the Court*

BRIDGES AND POETRY

by Bill Gutman
Brookfield, CT: Millbrook Press, 1992. 48p.

This book, illustrated with black-and-white and color photographs, will appeal to third- through fifth-grade readers. It is part of a series of books, Millbrook Sports World.

Earvin Johnson grew up as part of a large family in Lansing, Michigan. He was tall for his age when he started playing basketball in elementary school. He was 6 feet 5 inches in the ninth grade. In high school, he was given his nickname, Magic. When he left high school, he was 6 feet 8 inches and had the opportunity to go to many universities. He chose Michigan State.

On the Michigan State team, Magic was the point guard who did most of the ball handling. In 1978, his freshman year, Magic's team won the Big Ten Championship, and he was the only freshman named to the All American college team. In his sophomore year, Magic and his team won the finals of the National Collegiate Athletic Association (NCAA).

Magic Johnson decided to leave college and become a professional player. He was hired by the Los Angeles Lakers. He scored 26 points in his first professional game in 1979. That year in the National Basketball Association (NBA) playoffs, the Lakers won the championship, and Magic was named Most Valuable Player.

At age 32, Magic Johnson announced at the beginning of the 1991–92 season that he had contracted the HIV virus and would retire. He became a leader in the fight against AIDS. He also played in the NBA All Star game and was named Most Valuable Player in 1992.

Possible Topics for Further Investigation

1. When it was reported that Magic Johnson was HIV positive, there was much discussion about whether it would be safe for a player who was HIV positive to play with other people. Could other players contract this dangerous virus? If appropriate to the maturity of students, have a small group, with the help of a media specialist, research this topic and write a short paper, citing their sources of information, to share with the class.

2. When Magic Johnson played for Michigan State in 1978, his team, the Spartans, won the Big Ten Championship. Sometimes teams are added to or dropped from a league. Invite a small group of students to research the current teams of the Big Ten. Have the students show on a map of the United States where the Big Ten schools are located.

3. Two great basketball players, Magic Johnson and Larry Bird, played at the same time. In 1979, Larry Bird was named basketball's Player of the Year, even though Magic Johnson had led Michigan State to the NCAA title that year. When Magic Johnson led the Lakers to the NBA crown, he was not named Rookie of the Year—that award went to Larry Bird. Invite two students to study the careers and the basketball statistics of these two players throughout their entire careers and then share with the class the accomplishments of these men. (Charts might be used to present this information.) Have the class vote for which of the two they would select as the most outstanding basketball player, overall.

The Break Dance Kids: Poems of Sport, Motion, and Locomotion

by Lillian Morrison

New York: Lothrop, Lee & Shepard, 1985. 64p.

BRIDGES AND POETRY

This book of poetry, illustrated with black-and-white photographs, will appeal to students from kindergarten through fifth grade. The 35 poems touch on a variety of sports.

Of particular interest are the two poems about basketball. "Basketball Players" begins with a quotation from Bill Russell. It explores the idea of whether basketball players jump because they are happy or are happy because they jump. This 14-line poem makes use of end rhyme.

"Two Points" is a short poem. Some of the words are run together without spacing, and the poem takes the shape of a basketball net. The poem also makes use of two meanings of the word *clean*.

Many other sports are represented by one or more poems, including biking, dancing, skating, running, swimming, tennis, skiing, and baseball.

Some of the poems have a traditional shape, such as "B Boy." Others, such as "the swimmer" and "When I Read," explore the shape and sound of poetry. Students might need help to understand why the atypical poems are considered poems and not prose.

A few of the poems are social commentary, such as "Just for One Day." The inclusion of such poems shows readers how poetry, as well as essays, articles, and newspaper editorials, can make a statement about violence and contemporary life.

Discussion Starters and Multidisciplinary Activities

1 With a group of students, explore the poem "Sport" on page 15. The poem begins and ends with a single-word line. The other lines of the poem each contain two words, one of which is repeated from the previous line. What effect does this create?

2 "Morning Ringside" is a good poem for a class discussion. How does the poet use trees, wind, and birds in the poem to evoke the experience of a boxing match? How is the image of the boxing match carried through to the end of the poem?

3 Discuss with students the poem "Park Action." Identify each kind of action taking place in the park. Discuss the verbs used to create the action. What causes the jogger to become a sprinter?

4 The poems "Again and Again" and "Let's Go Mets" are about ballplayers who played for the Mets. Have a pair of students, with the help of a media specialist, research the Mets and share with the class what they learn. What was their hometown? How well did the Mets perform in the 1983 and 1984 seasons?

5 The poem "Kumina" is unusual. Ask a pair of students to research Kingston, Jamaica, and point it out to the class on a world map. After having researched Jamaica, can the students help the class with the meaning of the poem?

6 In the poem "Canoe and Ducks," the poet discusses mergansers. Have a pair of students research mergansers and either photocopy (with permission) or draw a picture of a merganser to share with the class.

Nonfiction Connections

📖 *Basketball's Greatest Players: The Year in Sports 1994*

📖 *Chicago Bulls*

📖 *Houston Rockets, Basketball Champions: The Year in Sports 1994*

📖 *Kareem Abdul-Jabbar*

📖 *Larry Bird*

📖 *Michael Jordan: Basketball to Baseball and Back*

📖 *Shaquille O'Neal*

📖 *Sports Great Dominique Wilkins*

📖 *The Story of Basketball*

📖 *Wilt Chamberlain*

📖 *The Young Basketball Player*

Basketball's Greatest Players: The Year in Sports 1994

NONFICTION CONNECTIONS

by Bob Italia
Minneapolis, MN: Abdo & Daughters, 1994. 32p.

This book is suitable for third- through fifth-grade readers. It is part of a sports reference series, The Year in Sports 1994, and is illustrated with color photographs.

This book explains the various basketball awards and how the recipients are selected. It examines the winners of various awards in professional basketball for the 1994 season. In the National Basketball Association (NBA), a 96-member panel of local and national professional basketball writers and broadcasters votes for most of the major awards. The NBA head coaches select the All-Rookie team and the All-Defensive team.

A few of the most important awards discussed in the book include the following:

The Most Valuable Player award for 1994 went to Houston Rockets center Hakeem Olajuwon, who won this award in his 10th professional season. Olajuwon was also selected as the 1994 Defensive Player of the Year (which he also won in 1993). The 1994 Rookie of the Year award went to Chris Webber of the Golden State Warriors, the youngest player in the league. The Sixth Man award in 1994 went to the Charlotte Hornets guard Dell Kurry. Lenny Wilkens, in his first season with the Atlanta Hawks, was selected as Coach of the Year in 1994.

A final section of this book pays tribute to Isaiah Thomas, chronicling his successful basketball career up to his retirement in May 1994.

Possible Topics for Further Investigation

1 Tracing the history of an important sports award can be an interesting research topic. Perhaps the most significant of basketball awards is the designation Most Valuable Player, which is usually awarded to players with high scoring averages. Have a few interested students research the history of this award, which is named after Maurice Podoloff, the first commissioner of the NBA. The students should make a chart to share the information, showing the year of the award, the name of the player, and the name of the player's team.

2 Constellations are groups of stars, most of which are named after mythological personages, animals, and objects. Pegasus, the Winged Horse, and Orion, the Hunter, are two such constellations. Ask a group of interested students to do some "sports stargazing." Can they find groups of stars that seem to form the shape of a basketball player shooting a ball or a baseball player holding a bat? Have the students map the night sky on a sheet of paper and then "connect the dots" to create a sports constellation to share with the class.

3 The breathing rate of basketball players increases as their bodies need more oxygen. Perform some tests on willing classmates: Observe and record how many times they breathe per minute when sitting at their desks. How many times do they breathe per minute after 30 seconds of standing? After 30 seconds of running in place? Does everyone have the same breathing rate? Does the rate continue to increase after exercise?

Chicago Bulls

by Michael E. Goodman
Mankato, MN: Creative Education, 1993. 32p.

This book will appeal to third- through fifth-grade readers. It is illustrated with black-and-white and color photographs.

The author notes that Chicago is known for its size, for being a major industrial center, for the winds off Lake Michigan, and for its sporting teams, including the Chicago Bulls basketball team.

This book traces the history of professional basketball in Chicago, from the Chicago Bruins in 1925, to a revival of the Bruins in the 1940s, to the Gears in 1946, to the Stags in 1946–47, and to the Packers, who changed their name to the Zephyrs before the 1962–63 season. The latest franchise, the Bulls, began in 1966. In its first year, the new club made the National Basketball Association (NBA) playoffs.

For many years and through many coaches, the Bulls struggled, improved, declined, and improved again, but they were never a huge success. Then, in 1984, the team signed Michael Jordan. Almost immediately, attendance at games doubled. Air Jordan, as Michael Jordan was nicknamed, was a player who could drop a dunk shot, hit a long-range shot, steal a ball, and sail through the air. He brought in crowds.

During Jordan's first season with the Bulls, he led the team into the playoffs. They have made it to the playoffs every season since then. They came close to winning the championship many times. Finally, in the 1990–91 season, the Bulls won the NBA championship for the first time.

Possible Topics for Further Investigation

1   Chicago is often referred to as the Windy City. The winds that blow off Lake Michigan are strong and cold. Have a small group of students, with the help of a media specialist, research Chicago's weather to determine if Chicago really is one of the windiest and coldest cities in the United States. Where in the United States do the strongest wind gusts occur? Do some cities in the United States have consistently high winds? Based on average monthly temperatures, which cities in the United States are the coldest? Have students share with the class what they learn.

2   Invite a weather forecaster to visit the class and bring weather maps of the United States showing high and low temperatures. Ask the weather forecaster to explain the causes of high winds and also the wind-chill factor as related to the cold winds that blow off Lake Michigan. Another topic for a discussion of weather prediction might be the significance of a rising or falling barometer. Have students follow up the visit with a thank you letter to the guest.

3   When attendance at professional sporting events is low, advertising consultants are often called in to develop a campaign to arouse interest. Have a group of students brainstorm ideas that might increase attendance at the games of one of your state teams. Have the students share with the class their best three schemes and explain why these approaches would increase attendance. Have the class discuss whether the advertising techniques are promising.

Houston Rockets, Basketball Champions: The Year in Sports 1994

by Bob Italia
Minneapolis, MN: Abdo & Daughters, 1994. 32p.

This book is suitable for readers in grades three through five. It is illustrated with color photographs. While most books discuss techniques of the game or follow a basketball team through several years of college or professional ball, this book examines just one season, in detail.

The first section follows the Houston Rockets from early scouting reports to the regular season start in November and concludes with the final games in April. The second section describes the playoffs in Portland, Phoenix, and Utah.

The third section of the book chronicles the National Basketball Association (NBA) finals from game one through game seven, which the Houston Rockets won (they beat New York, 90-84), giving the city its first championship title. The Rockets' outstanding center, Hakeem Olajuwon, was named Most Valuable Player for the series.

By following one team through an entire season, the reader develops a sense of the ups and downs of the game. The Houston Rockets began their season in November with 15 consecutive wins but then found themselves in second place in mid-February, behind the San Antonio Spurs. By mid-April, they had clinched the division title.

The efforts of an entire season came down to a series of seven final championship games, the last of which the Rockets won by 6 points.

Possible Topics for Further Investigation

1. Hakeem Olajuwon and Shaquille O'Neal are outstanding centers. Each player will probably have fans in the classroom. Invite two students to research these players and determine why each deserves the title "outstanding center." The researchers should consider the following: In the years since the 1994 championship, how do these two players compare? Is there any other center who is as good as or better than Olajuwon and O'Neal? In recent seasons, how do the two compare in per-game averages for points, rebounds, and assists? In an oral presentation, have the students share with the class what they learn.

2. Basketball players have to keep in peak physical condition. They need to have strong bones and ligaments, the connective tissue that holds together the bones. One necessity for healthy bones is calcium. Have a student perform the following experiment to show the class that bones without calcium have less strength: Remove all the meat from a chicken leg bone and let it dry. Feel and examine the bone. Does it bend? Fill a small container with vinegar and immerse the bone for four days. Remove the bone, rinse it, and examine it again. How is it different? Will the bone break if bent? The acid in the vinegar has dissolved the calcium in the bone.

3. In a full season of regular games, playoffs, and championships, a team travels many miles. On a map of the United States, have a pair of students locate all the cities that the Houston Rockets visited during the 1993–94 season. How many miles is each of these cities from Houston?

📖 *Kareem Abdul-Jabbar*

by R. Thomas Cobourn
New York: Chelsea House, 1995. 112p.

This book is part of the Black Americans of Achievement series and will interest fourth- and fifth-grade readers. The text is illustrated with black-and-white photographs. An essay by Coretta Scott King serves as an introduction. The book is divided into nine chapters, each dealing with a phase of Kareem Abdul-Jabbar's career.

Chapter 1 chronicles Abdul-Jabbar's role in the 1985 National Basketball Association (NBA) championship series, in which, after a disappointing first game, Kareem led his team to victory.

Chapter 2 describes Kareem Abdul-Jabbar's youth and his basketball successes, beginning with seventh grade. Chapter 3 and Chapter 4 focus on his final years of high school and his decision to attend the University of California at Los Angeles (UCLA) in 1965. With Kareem Abdul-Jabbar playing center, the UCLA Bruins won three national championships.

Chapter 5 and Chapter 6 cover the period when Abdul-Jabbar boycotted the Olympic Games held in Mexico in 1968, protesting racial prejudice; converted to Islam; and signed with the Milwaukee Bucks.

Chapter 7 discusses Abdul-Jabbar's grief in 1973 when black Muslims murdered a family staying in a townhouse that he owned, his separation from his wife, physical injuries on the court, and his trade to the Los Angeles Lakers in 1975.

Chapter 8 describes how Abdul-Jabbar found new joy in basketball when joined by Magic Johnson, and how he rebuilt his personal life. The final chapter discusses the records Kareem Abdul-Jabbar established during his career.

Possible Topics for Further Investigation

1. Kareem Abdul-Jabbar's given name is Lew Alcindor. His parents were Catholic, and they sent their son to Catholic schools for part of his education. When Lew grew older, he converted to the Islamic religion and took a new name, Kareem Abdul-Jabbar. Have a small group of students, with the help of a media specialist, research the Islamic religion. What are its main tenets? How is an orthodox Muslim different from a black Muslim? In an oral presentation, have the students share with the class what they learn.

2. On page 105 is a full page of career statistics for Kareem Abdul-Jabbar. This page might be used as a source of math problems, as well as a practice exercise in reading and understanding numerical data presented in chart format. Discuss the page with students to help them understand how to interpret information from the chart. Have a group of students prepare a set of math story problems based on these statistics, including an answer key. Photocopy the story problems for the class to solve.

3. Kareem Abdul-Jabbar sustained two eye injuries during his professional career, after which he began using protective goggles. His first injury, in 1968, was a scratched cornea. Invite a local ophthalmologist to visit the class and bring either a model or charts showing the various parts of the eye. Ask the doctor to explain how the eye works. Before the visit, have students prepare questions for the doctor. Among these questions should be one about a scratched cornea. Have students follow up with a thank you letter to the guest.

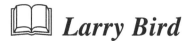 *Larry Bird*

by Sean Dolan
New York: Chelsea House, 1995. 64p.

NONFICTION CONNECTIONS

This book will appeal to third- through fifth-grade readers. It is part of a series of books, Basketball Legends.

Larry Joe Bird was born in 1956 in Bedford, Indiana. His family was poor, and he had a difficult childhood. His father couldn't hold a job for long; it was his mother who worked and kept the family together. When he was four, Larry Bird received his first basketball for Christmas. He played with his older brothers and sometimes practiced shooting alone on the school playground until the early morning hours. In his senior year, he grew 5 inches, to a height of 6 feet 7 inches.

Bird was recruited to Indiana University but stayed there just 24 days before returning home, where he got a job with the street department. The next fall, he entered Indiana State University. He did better in the smaller school but sat out his first year of basketball because he was considered a transfer student. In his senior year, he led his team to the finals. Though tempted by professional offers, he remained in college and earned his degree.

In his first year of professional basketball with the Boston Celtics, Bird was chosen Rookie of the Year. This was the first of many awards and successful years playing basketball. He (along with Magic Johnson) is credited with rekindling fans' interest in professional basketball. After winning a gold medal in the 1992 summer Olympic Games, Bird retired from basketball. Later he became a coach.

Possible Topics for Further Investigation

1. The average person greatly admires professional athletes, and these athletes sometimes earn enormous salaries. When Larry Bird began playing for the Boston Celtics, he was the highest-paid rookie in the history of the National Basketball Association (NBA). Have interested students, with the help of a media specialist, research the salaries of major sports figures in basketball, baseball, and football. The students should record their findings on a chart that can be displayed in the classroom. Ask other students to research the current salaries of your state's governor and the president. Compare these salaries in a class discussion.

2. Is Larry Bird or Magic Johnson the better basketball player? Organize two teams to research and then debate this question. Tell the teams that they need data to back up their opinions. When they are ready, ask the two teams to debate the issue before the class. Then have the class vote to determine which side won the debate. Also have class members give feedback to the debaters.

3. Have two students who are basketball fans attend a local game. Ask them to take notes and keep track of the total number of baskets attempted and scored on the court by one team and the number of free throws attempted and scored by two members of the team. Have the students share this information with the class. Have the class compute for each player the percentages of field goal and free throw attempts that were successful.

📖 *Michael Jordan: Basketball to Baseball and Back*

by Bill Gutman

Brookfield, CT: Millbrook Press, 1995. 49p.

This book is appropriate for third-through fifth-grade readers. It is illustrated with black-and-white and color photographs and is part of a series, Millbrook Sports World.

This book traces the life and participation in two sports of Michael Jordan, who was born in Brooklyn, New York, in 1963 but grew up in Wilmington, North Carolina. In high school, he played three sports but eventually gave up football and baseball and began playing basketball exclusively.

When Jordan entered the University of North Carolina in 1981, he was almost 6 feet 5 inches tall. As a freshman, he helped his team win the national championship. In his sophomore and junior years, Michael Jordan was named Player of the Year. In the summer of 1984, he made the U.S. Olympic team and helped them win a gold medal. Then he was drafted by the Chicago Bulls, scored a large number of points, and was named Rookie of the Year.

The next season, he broke his foot and sat out many games. In the seasons that followed, he set countless scoring records. In the 1990–91 season, he led the Bulls to the National Basketball Association (NBA) championship, a feat they repeated the next two seasons. He also helped the United States win another Olympic Games gold medal.

His father was murdered in 1993. Jordan briefly retired from basketball and tried professional baseball for 18 months, signing on with the Chicago White Sox in January 1994. When major league baseball players went on strike, Jordan retired from baseball and returned to the Chicago Bulls.

Possible Topics for Further Investigation

1. Sometimes, because of personal or physical problems, or simply from burnout, professional sports figures retire early. A few later attempt a comeback. Michael Jordan returned to the Chicago Bulls after 18 months and averaged 31.5 points in playoff games during his comeback year. Invite a small group of students to research major sports figures who retired early and later attempted a comeback. Were they successful or unsuccessful? In an oral presentation, have the students share with the class what they learn.

2. Air Jordan, as Michael Jordan is often called, is not the only great jumper. Grasshoppers can jump an incredible distance for their size. Collect a few grasshoppers (keep them in a fine-mesh cage with adequate food and water) and conduct a classroom experiment—"The Big Jump": Lay out a long sheet of newsprint and mark a starting line. Have a student place a grasshopper at the starting line and release it. Have "spotters" mark the spot to which the grasshopper jumps and "runners" catch the grasshopper. Repeat this with the other grasshoppers. Measure the distances jumped and compute the average distance. Measure the length of one of the grasshoppers. How many times their length did the grasshoppers jump horizontally? Ask students to convert this ratio to human scale. What distance would Michael Jordan be able to jump horizontally if he were a grasshopper? (Advise students on handling grasshoppers gently, and return the grasshoppers to their natural environment after the experiment.)

3. Michael Jordan is amazingly accurate when shooting a basketball. Invite interested students to try to express this in poetry. Post the poems on a classroom bulletin board.

📖 *Shaquille O'Neal*

by Edward Tallman
New York: Dillon Press, 1994. 72p.

This book, part of a series of biographies, will appeal to readers in grades three through five. It is illustrated with color photographs.

Shaquille O'Neal's father joined the army, so his family had to move several times, living in New Jersey, Georgia, and Germany. Perhaps because of the frequent moves and always being the new kid, Shaq (as he is often called) was often in trouble as a child. In eighth grade, though, he began to take responsibility for his life.

In 1987, Shaq finished his sophomore year of high school and moved with his family from Germany to San Antonio, Texas. He was successful at basketball as a high school student, so he had many options for college. He decided to go to Louisiana State University (LSU) in 1989 where he helped his team win two regular-season championships.

Because the "big three" of basketball (Michael Jordan, Magic Johnson, and Larry Bird) were getting older and retiring, the 1992 draft was especially important. The team that got first pick would undoubtedly choose Shaquille O'Neal, a 7-foot-1-inch, 304-pound basketball giant. The lucky team was the Orlando Magic, which quickly negotiated a seven-year, $41 million contract.

Shaq O'Neal has used his name and celebrity status to garner advertisement contracts with companies such as Reebok and Pepsi. By some, he is called an "action hero." He released a rap album, *Shaq Diesel*, in 1993. In 1994, he played a role in a basketball movie, *Blue Chips*, with Nick Nolte. With many career opportunities ahead, Shaq O'Neal continues to play at the level that has made him one of the greatest of current basketball stars.

Possible Topics for Further Investigation

1. Page 23 of the book suggests that basketball is a fluid and rhythmical game and that the teams of the 1980s and early 1990s could be classified according to kinds of music. The author suggests that the Boston Celtics of that time period were rock and roll—a soundtrack composed by Bruce Springsteen would have best expressed their playing style; the Los Angeles Lakers were sweet soul music; the Detroit Pistons exemplified gangsta rap; and the Chicago Bulls were hip-hop. Invite students to select a piece of music that they think expresses the playing style of a current basketball team. Have students bring the music to class, play a portion of it, and explain why they think the music expresses the team's playing style.

2. After reading this book, students will be aware of weaknesses that keep Shaquille O'Neal from being a "complete player." Have two students present a short skit to the class in which one plays a reporter and the other Shaquille O'Neal during an interview. Questions might include: How do you respond to statements that you pay more attention to movies and advertising than to basketball? How do you intend to change your performance at the free-throw line? "Shaquille" might answer seriously or humorously.

3. Shaquille O'Neal is a passionate rap fan. Invite two students who are rap fans to write an original rap about a game of basketball. Have them set the rap to music, record it, and share it with the class.

📖 *Sports Great Dominique Wilkins*

NONFICTION CONNECTIONS

by Peter C. Bjarkman
Springfield, NJ: Enslow, 1996. 64p.

This book is appropriate for third-through fifth-grade readers. It is part of a series, Sports Great Books, and is illustrated with black-and-white photographs.

The author begins his discussion of Dominique Wilkins by describing the final game of the 1988 Eastern Conference semifinal playoff series, which pitted two great forwards against each other: Larry Bird of the Boston Celtics and Dominique Wilkins of the Atlanta Hawks. Although the Celtics beat the Hawks 118-116, Wilkins scored 47 points.

Dominique Wilkins's father was a soldier stationed in France, so Dominique lived in France for the first 12 years of his life. His favorite game there was marbles. He started playing basketball in high school after moving with his mother from France back to North Carolina. Everyone wanted Dominique Wilkins to play basketball at North Carolina State, but Wilkins chose to move to Georgia.

Dominique Wilkins had three great years with the University of Georgia and then decided to leave college and enter the National Basketball Association (NBA) draft. He was traded to the Atlanta Hawks and became an NBA superstar. He is one of a small group of basketball players to accumulate more than 25,000 career points.

Dominique Wilkins eventually played for the Boston Celtics but left them in 1995 and signed a $7 million contract to play for a basketball team in Greece. He led the Greek team to the European Cup Championship.

Possible Topics for Further Investigation

1 Dominique Wilkins faced many disappointments during his career. He thought that he deserved to be on the Olympic Dream Team, which won a gold medal, but he wasn't selected. He had to make a comeback from a bad heel injury that threatened his career. The Atlanta Hawks traded him to the Los Angeles Clippers for a younger player. Invite interested students to write an original sports short story in which one of the characters faces and overcomes a terrible disappointment. Allow time for students to share their stories with the class.

2 When this book was published in 1996, Dominique Wilkins invited people to write him c/o Panathinaikos, Satovriandov 19, 10431, Athens, Greece. Ask two interested students to write a letter to Dominique Wilkins requesting a photo or autograph for the classroom bulletin board. The students should include with their request IRCs (international return coupons). A post office will advise them of a sufficient amount to cover the return postage and a self-addressed envelope. Have the students share any response with the class.

3 Consult the chart on page 62, which shows the career statistics of Dominique Wilkins. Ask a small group of students to prepare 10 math questions (including an answer key) that can be answered using the numerical data found in the graph. Photocopy the problems and distribute them to the class. Have students refer to the chart, estimate answers, and then solve the problems. Review the answers in class, having students explain how they solved each problem. (There may be several correct approaches to solving a problem.)

📖 *The Story of Basketball*

by Dave Anderson
New York: William Morrow, 1988. 182p.

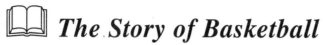

NONFICTION CONNECTIONS

This book will appeal to fourth- and fifth-grade readers. It is illustrated with black-and-white photographs. *The Story of Basketball* introduces the reader to famous players and coaches of the past, as well as the present, and along the way provides insights into basketball fundamentals—shooting, passing, rebounding, and defense.

Part One is divided into five sections: 1920–1935 deals with the original Boston Celtics and the Harlem Globetrotters; 1935–1955 discusses the development of the game under the influence of Hank Luisetti and George Mikan; 1955–1965 shows the effect on the game of two outstanding players, Bill Russell and Wilt Chamberlain; 1965–1975 is devoted to John Wooden's dynasty at the University of California at Los Angeles

(UCLA); and in the period since 1975, the author discusses the influence on basketball of players such as Larry Bird and Magic Johnson.

Part Two is also divided into six sections: shooting, including the sky hook and the jumper; passing, emphasizing how even a 5-foot-7-inch player can be effective on the court; defense, describing in detail the effect on the game of a player who can block shots; rebounding, discussing position and timing; coaching and how good coaches create the environment in which their players can develop talent and succeed; and "Why Is Basketball So Popular?" stressing that basketball is a simple game, requiring little equipment, that can be played by both men and women.

Possible Topics for Further Investigation

1. The United States boycotted the Olympic Games in 1980 and 1984. Have a group of interested students, with the help of a media specialist, research this topic. What is a boycott? Why did the United States boycott the games in 1980 and 1984? Did any other countries boycott those games? Were the games held in spite of the boycott? Have the Olympic Games been boycotted in other years? Have the students share their findings with the class.

2. Basketball survived the "1951 point-fixing scandal," which involved some of the nation's best college teams and players. Ask a pair of students to research this scandal in the school or public library using microfiche reproductions of newspapers. Have the students photocopy the newspaper articles to share with the class in an oral presentation about the scandal.

3. The Harlem Globetrotters are a group of basketball players who have performed in nearly 100 countries before millions of people. They have a long and interesting history. Have a small group of students, with the help of a media specialist or an adult volunteer, research the topic and prepare for the class a presentation highlighting interesting facts about the team. Why are they called the Harlem Globetrotters? When was the team founded? Who are some of their famous players? When did they first add a woman to the team? Are they still performing?

From *Exploring the World of Sports*. © 1998 Phyllis J. Perry. Teacher Ideas Press. (800) 237-6124.

📖 *Wilt Chamberlain*

NONFICTION CONNECTIONS

by Ron Frankl

New York: Chelsea House, 1995. 64p.

This book, part of the series Basketball Legends, will appeal to fourth- and fifth-grade readers. It is illustrated with black-and-white photographs.

Choosing a few people to study from a huge number of remarkably fine basketball players means identifying what makes a player a legend or a superstar. The introduction to this book explains how superstars distinguish themselves.

This book chronicles the career of Wilt Chamberlain, a basketball legend. Records he set have yet to be equaled, including averaging 50 points per game for an entire season. Chamberlain was a huge man, but he was fast and could run, jump, and pass, as well as shoot. He played center and was an exceptional rebounder. In one professional game, he pulled down 55 rebounds.

Perhaps his most amazing record was set in 1962 when he scored 100 points in a single game while playing with the Philadelphia Warriors.

Chamberlain played collegiate basketball for the Jayhawks at Kansas University. In his first year on the varsity team, the Jayhawks won the conference championship. Chamberlain left the university at the end of his junior year and spent a year playing for the Harlem Globetrotters. He began his National Basketball Association (NBA) career by joining the Philadelphia Warriors for the 1959–60 year. In his first season, Chamberlain was named Rookie of the Year and the NBA's Most Valuable Player and was chosen for the All-NBA team. He continued playing remarkable basketball for 14 seasons in the NBA.

Possible Topics for Further Investigation

1. Page 61 of this book is filled with statistics. Have a small group of students study this page and prepare a set of math story problems (including an answer key) for the class to solve. The level of difficulty will be determined by the age and skill level of the students involved. Students should write out the problems and solve them individually; then they should share the problems within the group and check them for accuracy. A typical story problem might be: If Wilt Chamberlain attempted 1,377 field goals during the 1967–68 season and scored 819 of his shots, what percentage of his attempted field goals were successful? Answer: 59.5 percent.

2. Wilt Chamberlain was exceptionally tall. Students might want to research height in families. Have a small group of students obtain accurate height measurements for families of relatives, friends, and neighbors. For each family, students will need the height of the mother, the father, and all the grown children. Students might determine for this sampling of families whether children are the same height as, taller than, or shorter than parents.

3. Have a group of students make a collage, "Outstanding Centers," and hang it in the classroom. They will first need to find photographs of such superstar basketball centers as Wilt Chamberlain, Kareem Abdul-Jabbar, Hakeem Olajuwon, Patrick Ewing, David Robinson, and Shaquille O'Neal. These photographs might be cut out from newspapers or magazines and then arranged into an attractive design.

The Young Basketball Player

**NONFICTION
CONNECTIONS**

by Chris Mullin, with Brian Coleman
New York: Dorling Kindersley, 1995. 45p.

This book will appeal to readers in grades three through five. It is a large-format book with color, action photographs throughout.

Chris Mullin draws on his experience with the Golden State Warriors in the National Basketball Association (NBA) to introduce basic basketball skills, advanced techniques, and team tactics. In describing the basic equipment and clothes needed, the author stresses the importance of shoes.

A two-page spread is used to show and describe aspects of the sport such as the basketball court and court markings, the backboard and shot clock, game duration, overtime, charged time-outs, substitutes, and the duties of various basketball officials during the game.

In teaching basics such as dribbling, driving in to score, and passing, the book relies on photographic sequences and clear step-by-step instructions. Photographs depict both boys and girls playing the game.

The section on shooting skills explains the set shot, the layup, the jump shot, the hook shot, and the slam dunk. There is a section on the importance of rebounds.

The defensive skills discussed include defending against a dribbler, guarding a passer, and playing positions. Other strategies include the fast break, give and go, and screen play. The book also contains rules, a glossary, and addresses that might be helpful in securing additional information.

Possible Topics for Further Investigation

1 In 1992, the author of this book, Chris Mullin, was a member of the Dream Team that played basketball in the Olympic Games in Barcelona, Spain. That was the first year professional basketball players were allowed to compete in the games, and the United States won the gold medal. Have a pair of students, with the help of a media specialist, research the Olympic basketball games of 1992. Which players represented the United States? Which countries did the United States play? Which country won the silver medal? The bronze medal?

2 Approximately 200 countries are affiliated with the International Basketball Federation (FIBA). The rules of the FIBA differ slightly from those of the NBA in the United States and from those of the National Collegiate Athletic Association (NCAA), or the American College League. Have a small group of students make notes from the book on the differences and then explain them to the class. For example, in the FIBA, the offensive team must take a shot within 30 seconds of gaining possession of the ball. In the NBA, players have only 24 seconds; in the NCAA, players have 35 seconds.

3 Have a pair of interested students, with the help of an adult volunteer or a media specialist, research the beginnings of basketball, as originated in 1891 by Dr. James Naismith, who taught at the YMCA International Training School in Massachusetts. How and why did basketball spread from its early beginnings? Have the students write a report, using at least three sources (cited in a bibliography), to share with the class.

From *Exploring the World of Sports.* © 1998 Phyllis J. Perry. Teacher Ideas Press. (800) 237-6124.

Part III
Football

Football

● FICTION ●

- *Benjy the Football Hero*
- *The Berenstain Bears and the Female Fullback*
- *Blindside Blitz*
- *Breaking Loose*
- *The Dallas Titans Get Ready for Bed*

- *The Dog That Stole Football Plays*
- *Forward Pass*
- *Game Plan*
- *The Great Quarterback Switch*
- *Just for Kicks*
- *Matt's Crusade*

◆ BRIDGES AND POETRY ◆

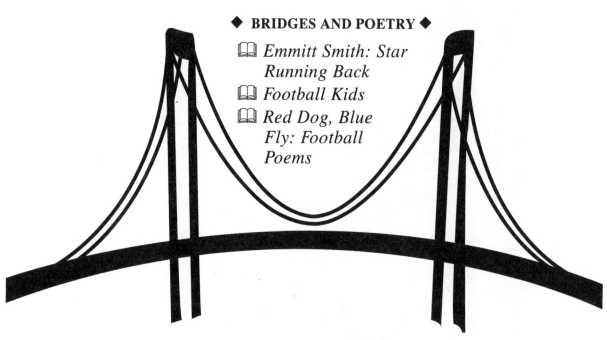

- *Emmitt Smith: Star Running Back*
- *Football Kids*
- *Red Dog, Blue Fly: Football Poems*

■ NONFICTION CONNECTIONS ■

- *Barry Sanders: Rocket Running Back*
- *The Best Players: The Year in Sports 1994*
- *The First Book of Football*
- *Football*
- *Jerry Rice*

- *Joe Montana*
- *Joe Namath*
- *Steve Young: Star Quarterback*
- *The Super Book of Football*
- *Walter Payton*
- *William Perry: The Refrigerator*

—OTHER TOPICS TO EXPLORE—

—blitz	—recruitment	—signals	—stadiums
—bowl games	—red shirt	—sports injuries	—statistics
—kickers	—referees	—sports medicine	—T-formation

From *Exploring the World of Sports*. © 1998 Phyllis J. Perry. Teacher Ideas Press. (800) 237-6124.

Football

● *Fiction* ●

- Benjy the Football Hero
- The Berenstain Bears and the Female Fullback
- Blindside Blitz
- Breaking Loose
- The Dallas Titans Get Ready for Bed
- The Dog That Stole Football Plays
- Forward Pass
- Game Plan
- The Great Quarterback Switch
- Just for Kicks
- Matt's Crusade

63

📖 *Benjy the Football Hero*

FICTION

by Jean Van Leeuwen
New York: Dial Books for Young Readers, 1985. 168p.

This book, illustrated with a few black-and-white drawings, will appeal to second- and third-grade readers. It is told from the viewpoint of a fourth-grade boy named Benjy.

Benjy decides to hold a football birthday party on the first Saturday after the start of the school year. The party turns out well. Even Benjy's little sister, Melissa, doesn't cause a disaster. In the birthday game, Benjy makes a 90-yard run for a touchdown, and he dreams of becoming a football hero.

Benjy has a hard time deciding how to spend his birthday money when his mother agrees to take him shopping. Little Melissa adds considerable excitement to the shopping trip when she keeps getting into things.

Benjy finally decides on a Dallas Cowboys sweatshirt, which he wears home even though it is too big for him.

Benjy and other kids in his class begin playing football at recess against the other fourth-grade class, led by Alex Crowley. Benjy's team is helped by a transfer student, Case, the Ace, and by a girl, Killer Kelly, both of whom are good football players.

Benjy makes a foolish bet, his Cowboys shirt against a Cowboys football helmet, that Benjy's team can win the fourth-grade "Super Bowl." There are obstacles to overcome, such as being denied recess by the teachers, and poison ivy, which strikes Case, the Ace, but Benjy's team, by using their brains instead of relying only on brawn, succeed in winning the big game.

Discussion Starters and Multidisciplinary Activities

1 Benjy's little sister, Melissa, sometimes causes him problems, such as cutting short his birthday shopping trip. Allow students time to discuss Melissa's activities and how they think Benjy really feels about his little sister.

2 Invite students to discuss which of the fourth-graders described in the book is the person they would most want like for a friend. Why?

3 The other fourth-grade class immediately asked for a rematch after losing the fourth-grade Super Bowl. Benjy and his friends declined. Ask students to discuss who they think would have won a rematch. Why?

4 Benjy takes his little sister, Melissa, trick-or-treating with him. Invite a pair of interested students to research the origins of Halloween. Where, when, and why did trick-or-treating begin? Have the students share this information with the class.

5 Case comes down with a bad case of poison ivy. Have a small group of students research this topic. They should make a sketch and color it to show what a poison ivy plant looks like. They should also research what causes the rash and popular remedies. Have the students share this information with the class.

6 Benjy does not like scary movies. Students may have mixed feelings on this topic. Have two students conduct a survey to determine what the class thinks is the most frightening current television series. Have the students make a bar graph showing the results of their survey to share with the class.

The Berenstain Bears and the Female Fullback

 FICTION

by Stan Berenstain and Jan Berenstain
New York: Random House, 1993. 102p.

Part of a popular series, this Big Chapter Book will appeal to students in kindergarten through grade three. There are comical black-and-white illustrations throughout.

The story begins at the opening of a new school year. Brother is excited about being the quarterback of the football team and Sister is planning to be a cheerleader. Papa is thrilled about his son's plans, but Mama is angry that Papa doesn't seem as interested in his daughter's accomplishments.

At school, Brother and Sister learn that Queenie McBear is planning some changes at Bear Country School. For one thing, she has decided to run for student body president. She wants to change the way that boys and girls are treated at the school. Brother is also running for student body president.

When it's time for football tryouts, Coach "Bullhorn" Grizzmeyer won't let Bertha Broom try out for the team. Brother is not happy with the way Bertha is treated.

Controversy spreads throughout Bear Country, with some parents believing that Bertha should be given a chance to be on the football team and others thinking that football is not a game for girls. Brother suggests that they give Bertha a tryout to stop the controversy. Bertha makes the team.

To break the election tie, Brother offers to let Queenie be president. Queenie makes a good president, Brother has a good year as quarterback, and Bertha is a fine fullback.

Discussion Starters and Multidisciplinary Activities

1. The character in the story who changed the most was Too-Tall. Have students discuss what he did and how he changed from the beginning to the end of the story.

2. On page 100, Sister talks about a male chauvinist. Have students discuss this topic. What is a male chauvinist? Point out the examples of male chauvinism that appear throughout the book.

3. Ask students to discuss what they would have done if they were Queenie and the election results were tied? Would they have accepted the presidency from Brother? Why?

4. Have two students conduct a survey to determine how boys' interests are different from girls' interests. Have the students choose six popular television programs. Print a ballot for each student that lists the six programs and asks students to rank the programs from 1 (most favorite) to 6 (least favorite). Compile the results for the entire class, for boys, and for girls. Discuss the results and whether there are significant differences for boys and girls.

5. Invite a small group of students to cut out for one month all the articles in a local newspaper's sports section that feature local high school teams. Have the students share with the class the number of articles, the percentage of articles that covered boys' sporting events, and the percentage of articles that covered girls' sporting events. Discuss with the class any difference in percentages.

6. There are constellations of stars called the Big Bear (Ursa Major) and the Little Bear (Ursa Minor). Invite a group of students to research the mythologies and legends about these constellations. Have the students share the stories with the class and explain when and where these constellations can be seen in the night sky.

📖 *Blindside Blitz*

FICTION

by David Halecroft
New York: Puffin Books, 1991. 118p.

This book is part of the Alden All Stars series. It will appeal to readers in grades three through five. The plot is straightforward, with realistic sports action.

The main character is Matt Greene, a running back for Alden Junior High's eighth-grade football team, the Panthers. As Matt and his friends practice football before the school year begins, they are already looking forward to their first game. Matt's friend, Jesse, is the quarterback.

During their first school-season scrimmage, the boys worry about Anderson, the middle linebacker on the Williamsport team. Anderson is big and has been known to blitz the quarterback. Jesse is hurt on a late hit by Anderson and is taken to the hospital. The Alden Panthers lose, 14-13.

Even worse, they learn that Jesse has a fractured ankle and will be out for much of the season.

Coach Litzinger decides that Matt is the best natural athlete on the team and can be taught to be the substitute quarterback. Matt doesn't like this because he wants to enjoy his year as a running back. He does his best and begins to like being quarterback. Jesse gets mad, thinking that Matt is trying to take over his position.

Jesse recovers in time to play the championship game against Williamsport. This time Matt is injured, but an X-ray reveals no broken ribs, so he returns to play the final minutes of the last quarter: Jesse throws a pass to Matt to win the game.

Discussion Starters and Multidisciplinary Activities

1 Jesse and Matt can't agree on which position on the football team is the most important. Ask students to discuss which position they think is the most important. Why?

2 After a time, Matt begins to enjoy playing quarterback. Ask students to discuss situations in which they have been pressured to try something that they really didn't want to do and then discovered that they liked. How and why did they eventually begin to enjoy the activity?

3 When the boys see an old news clip showing Big Bill, Matt's father, being tackled by number 66, the same number that Anderson has on the Williamsport team, those who are superstitious think that Matt has been jinxed—the same thing will happen to him in the game. Ask students to discuss superstitions. Do any of them do something or wear something such as a lucky pair of socks to help them win a game?

4 Invite students to write an original short story about a football game. They may illustrate their stories if desired. Post the stories on a classroom bulletin board.

5 Using a computer and crossword puzzle software, or simply using graph paper, have a pair of students prepare a football crossword puzzle (including clues and an answer key) for the class to solve. Photocopy the puzzle for the class.

6 Jesse fractured his ankle. Ask a pair of students to use reference books from home or from the library to research the human ankle and make a diagram. They should label the various parts. Hang the diagram on a classroom bulletin board.

From *Exploring the World of Sports.* © 1998 Phyllis J. Perry. Teacher Ideas Press. (800) 237-6124.

📖 *Breaking Loose*

by David Halecroft
New York: Puffin Books, 1990. 114p.

This book, part of the Alden All Stars series, will appeal to third- through fifth-grade readers. It is not illustrated.

A group of boys who have been best friends for years and have enjoyed playing football with any number of players in parks and backyards, find themselves ready to begin seventh grade at Alden Junior High and join a "real" football team. Faced with this situation, the boy who changes most is Matt Greene. Matt's father is a retired National Football League (NFL) star, and Matt is desperately trying to live up to his father's expectations.

Matt becomes very serious and is unwilling to joke with his former friends Josh, Jesse, and Woody. He doesn't have time to go to the Game Place or drink sodas. For Matt, everything is about serious football.

Perhaps because he is trying too hard, Matt constantly makes mistakes on the field whenever his father is watching or videotaping the team, and then his father points out Matt's errors. Matt's attitude turns his teammates against him, and he no longer feels joyful about playing football.

Coach Wright has a talk with Matt and with his father. As a consequence, Matt's father stops pressuring him, and immediately, Matt's playing improves. Matt apologizes to his teammates and begins to play great football. By the time the Alden Junior High team faces its final championship game, they have developed enough skill and team spirit to carry them to victory.

Discussion Starters and Multidisciplinary Activities

1. Have students discuss the various factors that are putting so much pressure on Matt to perform brilliantly on the football field. Which of these factors can be attributed to Matt's father?

2. Josh and Matt lose their friendship for a while. During this period, Josh is particularly hard on Matt. Have students discuss what Josh says and does to hurt Matt.

3. Coach Wright is an interesting character. Have students discuss whether they would like to have him for a coach. Why?

4. Big Bill autographed the footballs he gave away. Autographed balls can be valuable. Invite students to research the value of balls from various sports that are autographed by current star athletes and share with the class what they learn.

5. In the championship game, two missed field-goal attempts were significant. Have a pair of interested students research Super Bowl games. Have any games been won or lost by a field goal? Have the students share with the class what they learn.

6. Coach Wright emphasized physical training for his team. Ask students to do an experiment: Take your pulse while you are sitting calmly and quietly. Record the pulse in beats per minute. On a staircase, step onto a first step with your right foot and then your left foot. Step down with your right foot and then your left foot. Repeat for 30 seconds. Sit down and take your pulse. Record your pulse every minute. How long does it take for your pulse to return to normal?

The Dallas Titans Get Ready for Bed

FICTION

by Karla Kuskin
illustrated by Marc Simont
New York: Harper & Row, 1986. 42p.

Second- and third-grade readers will enjoy this easy-to-read text and its humorous pictures. Surprisingly, this story begins just as a football game ends. It tells what happens in the locker room after the game.

The Dallas Titans have just won a big game. Players are being carried on their teammates' shoulders. Fans are smiling and crying with happiness. Everyone heads for the locker room, which becomes crowded with players, relatives, coaches, and doctors. Reporters and photographers are taking notes and pictures. The owner and the coach talk to the team. The coach never smiles; he tells the team that they have practice the next morning and they should get into the showers and go to bed as quickly as they can.

The players remove a lot of equipment before taking their showers. Some players help the others. In addition to their football jerseys and socks, they are wearing padding, extra socks, tape, and so on. Some players are neat and tidy, putting their soiled things in a laundry bin. Others toss things haphazardly around the locker room. The floor of the locker room disappears beneath their clothes.

After they have showered, the team members put on their street clothes and go home. Some have a snack—and others eat more than that—before they finally go to bed. They sleep and dream about the next big game.

Discussion Starters and Multidisciplinary Activities

1. The coach in this story is called Dutch Scorch. He never smiles. Ask students if they have a favorite coach of some sport they enjoy. What is the coach's name? Does he or she have a nickname? If students could name the coach in this book, what name might they choose?

2. The owner of the team tells the players that their upcoming game is important. She promises them a tremendous party if they win. Have students discuss why the players didn't get a party after winning this important game.

3. Zelinka's little brother is with him in the locker room. At the end of the story, when it is time to go home, the little brother is missing. Ask students to suggest where he might be.

4. Invite a coach from a local high school team to visit the class and bring a football uniform (rib pads, elbow pads, shoulder pads, face mask, helmet, tape, shoes, etc.). Have the coach explain how and why each piece of the uniform is used and how it helps to protect the player.

5. Pages 28 and 29 contain much information about socks. Invite four students to reread those pages and then write a series of math story problems (including an answer key) based on the 45 players in the locker room. Photocopy the problems for the class to solve.

6. Jones, number 12, threw the winning touchdown pass to Blimp, number 17. Ask a few interested students to draw a new illustration for the book—a depiction of the pass that won the football game. Students may use any medium they prefer. Post the illustrations in the classroom.

From *Exploring the World of Sports*. © 1998 Phyllis J. Perry. Teacher Ideas Press. (800) 237-6124.

FICTION

📖 *The Dog That Stole Football Plays*

by Matt Christopher
illustrated by Bill Ogden
Boston: Little, Brown, 1980. 48p.

This easy-to-read book will appeal to students in first through third grades. There are many humorous black-and-white illustrations.

When Mike sees the Airedale dog that is for sale in the pet shop, he finds that he and the dog share telepathy. Mike can tell what the dog is thinking, and the Airedale, Harry, knows what Mike is thinking.

Mike buys Harry, and although the two can communicate with each other, they keep their telepathy a secret. Harry asks Mike to take him to football game. Mike is worried that his dog will get into trouble, but finally he relents and takes Harry to the game.

Harry sits on the sidelines and overhears the coach of the opposing team sending in instructions for each play of the game. Harry sends his thoughts to Mike, so Mike and his team, the Jets, are ready for every play. The opponents can't gain yardage, and often lose ground. Mike's team wins easily.

This happens for a number of games. Mike begins to worry that maybe this isn't fair, but he wants his team to win, so Mike and Harry continue. On the day of an important game, Harry is at home sick. The Jets play poorly during the first half, and it looks like they'll lose. Then Mike stirs up his team to fight and win. When Harry appears, Mike insists on not receiving help. The Jets win fair and square.

Discussion Starters and Multidisciplinary Activities

1. Have students discuss whether they think it was fair that Mike helped the Jets win games by using telepathy to learn what plays the opposing team was planning.

2. Have students discuss whether they would like to own a pet with whom they could communicate using telepathy. What would be the advantages? What might be the disadvantages?

3. Mike's father played an important role in this story. Have students discuss what Mike's father did that was crucial to allow the Jets to tie the final football game.

4. Students who can't communicate through telepathy might enjoy communicating with a simple telephone. Have two students demonstrate an experiment: Punch a small hole into the center of the bottoms of two empty plastic margarine tubs. Pass a 12-foot string through the two holes and knot the string at each end so that it won't pull out of the tubs. One student holds a tub over his or her ear while the other student pulls the string taut and whispers into the other cup. The string carries the sound as vibrations and then transforms the vibrations back to sound.

5. The illustration on the cover of this book shows a dog running onto the field with a sheet of football plays hanging around its neck. This does not happen in the story. Encourage students to design a new cover, showing how Harry really steals the plays.

6. Invite two students to act out a short scene in which Harry and Mike talk together, showing the different perspectives of dog and human. Perhaps Harry has chased a cat or Mike has sneaked a cookie. What will each character say to the other?

📖 *Forward Pass*

FICTION

by Thomas J. Dygard
New York: Morrow Junior Books, 1989. 186p.

This story with a high school setting will appeal to fifth-grade readers. The main character in the story is an athletic girl who is recruited to play the position of pass receiver on the boys' football team.

Jill Winston is a star basketball player on the high school team. Her father and her older brother played on the school football team. When the coach realizes that he has no one who can consistently catch his quarterback's passes, he decides to approach Jill. He explains that she will be used only in the end zone or where she can quickly step out of bounds on the sidelines so that there will be minimal danger of tackling and injury. The coach convinces Jill and persuades her parents and her boyfriend to let her give it a try.

Jill proves to be a secret weapon. Often she catches passes. Sometimes she just serves as a decoy. Both ways she's effective. Although many protests are made, and the media turns the girl football player into front-page news, Jill, her coach, and the other players come through it all in fine fashion.

Just before the championship game, Jill makes the decision to quit football after the game and return to the basketball team. She shares this news only with her parents. She plays in the game, makes a tackle, and catches a touchdown pass that wins the game. The following week, she tells the coach and team of her decision, confident that they can continue to win, without her.

Discussion Starters and Multidisciplinary Activities

1 The coach decides to keep Jill's entry into football a secret from almost everyone. Only Jill's parents, her boyfriend, and the quarterback know. Have students discuss whether they think this was wise. What might have happened if other players, coaches, and the newspapers had known about it before her first game?

2 Jill's mother was more willing to let Jill play on the football team than Jill's father was. Have students discuss why they think this was so.

3 Ask students to discuss how they thought the football team in general, and Lenny Parker, the wide receiver, in particular, would take the news that a girl had been added to the team.

4 This story mentions "the president of the North Central Conference." This group determined whether it was acceptable for a girl to play on the football team. Invite a pair of students to research what group governs high school football in your area. What rules do they have and how do these rules affect school sports? Have the students share with the class what they learn.

5 How do football shoes differ from shoes used in baseball and in track and field? Have a pair of students bring to class a pair of each of the three types of athletic shoes, point out the differences, and explain why each type is designed the way it is.

6 Jill's expertise in basketball helps in football games, but the playing areas are quite different. Ask a pair of students to research the following: the length and width of a standard basketball court and the height of the basket; and the length and width of a standard football field, the height of the crossbar on the goalpost, and the distance between the two posts on one goalpost.

📖 *Game Plan*

● FICTION

by Thomas J. Dygard
New York: Morrow Junior Books, 1993. 220p.

This book will appeal to fourth- and fifth-grade readers. It is not illustrated. The central character is Beano Hatton, student manager for a small high school football team in northeast Indiana.

Beano is small and not very athletic, but he has worked with Coach Pritchard as the student manager throughout his high school years. When the Coach is badly injured in an automobile accident the week before the last football game of the year, the school principal tries to find an adult replacement. Everyone has a good excuse, so in desperation, the principal asks Beano to take over.

As a student, Beano is always prepared and organized. He brings these same traits to coaching the Barton High Tigers. He calls coaches of other teams who have played the Carterville Bobcats to learn as much as he can about his opponents.

Beano's main problem is the team quarterback, Marty Tucker. Marty sees no reason for taking advice on plays from Beano. Instead, he chooses to challenge or ignore Beano as the team goes through its last few days of practice before the final game.

Finally, Marty quits the team. Beano fears others may follow, but no one does. So Beano works with the sophomore quarterback, Dave Harris. Dave proves to have a good long pass and is eager to try. Finding that he's not indispensable, Marty comes back to Beano and says he'd like to rejoin the team.

Beano's game plan works beautifully and he is able to use both quarterbacks in winning the final game.

Discussion Starters and Multidisciplinary Activities

1   Have students discuss the interactions between Beano and the football players that show Beano has many of the characteristics of a good coach.

2   Have students discuss whether they were surprised when Marty and Dave exchanged "high fives" during the game?

3   In what ways did the various adults (Beano's father, the principal, Mr. Custer, the coaches that Beano called on the phone, the sports writer) show their confidence in Beano and try to help him in his role of football coach?

4   Have students role play the meeting between Coach Pritchard and Beano in the hospital on Saturday after the big game. What will the coach want to ask Beano? What will Beano offer as highlights of the game? Will either of them have questions for the other?

5   Aside from the illustration on the cover, this is a book without illustrations. Invite interested students to illustrate scenes from the book using any medium they prefer. Have students note the page of the book where they would insert the illustration. Display the pictures in the classroom.

6   A local sports writer could take many approaches to a newspaper story about the final football game in the story. Ask students to study the sports section of a local newspaper and then write a sports article about the game between the Barton High Tigers and the Carterville Bobcats. Students should include a headline. Post the stories on a classroom bulletin board.

The Great Quarterback Switch

FICTION

by Matt Christopher
Boston: Little, Brown, 1984. 97p.

This book will appeal to third- through fifth-grade readers. The major characters are twins who play on a junior high football team.

Michael was hit by a car and is confined to a wheelchair for the rest of his life. His twin brother, Tom, is a quarterback on the Eagles football team. At each game, Michael tries to communicate the plays he would call to his brother by using ESP.

The boys have a neighbor, Ollie, who explains to them TEC (thought-energy control). He says that if they concentrate and wish hard enough, the boys will be able to switch places. This would, in essence, allow Michael to play again and would also give Tom a breather when he has been playing hard.

The boys do their best and succeed at TEC in a game against the Scorpions. Michael goes in long enough to make a touchdown. The boys now realize that they can use TEC whenever they both want.

There are problems, though. Two girls hang around Tom and Michael. Tom is afraid to speak to them because he thinks that they may recognize that he is not really Michael. Michael is equally afraid that Tom's teammates will be able to tell that he is not really Tom. Still, the boys are careful and inventive, and Michael is able to play again, making passes and touchdowns and giving Tom a rest when he needs it. Michael feels the thrill of playing, and Tom comes to appreciate what life in a wheelchair is like.

Discussion Starters and Multidisciplinary Activities

1   At first, Vickie and Carol appear to be unlikely friends. In time, though, Michael comes to recognize their strengths. Have students discuss what attributes Vickie and Carol share.

2   Have students discuss what problems might arise if Tom and Michael began using TEC in situations off the football field.

3   Michael tried to talk to his father once about ESP, but he thought that his father wasn't really interested and was only being polite. Ask students to discuss what his father said or did (or failed to say or do) that gave Michael this impression.

4   Ollie was happy to have found two boys who sometimes visited and talked with him. They helped him feel less lonely. Have a group of students check with a local nursing or retirement home to see if they can take part in some project for the elderly. Perhaps they could make decorations or table centerpieces for a Thanksgiving or Christmas dinner, present a play, or sing carols.

5   ESP is an interesting topic. Have a small group of students, with the help of a media specialist, research ESP experiments that have been conducted under controlled scientific conditions. Have the students share with the class what they learn.

6   One type of injury that sometimes results in paralysis is a spinal cord injury. Have an interested pair of students research the spinal cord and its function within the body. Have the students share with the class what they learn.

FICTION

📖 *Just for Kicks*

by Paul Baczewski
New York: J. B. Lippincott, 1990. 183p.

This book will appeal to fourth- and fifth-grade readers. It is not illustrated. The central character is 15-year-old Brandon Lewis.

Brandon lives with two brothers and a sister who are all jocks. His siblings play hard, eat a lot, and push around their brother. Brandon is always coming up with bright ideas. His idea this fall is to have his sister, Sarah, fill the only weakness in the varsity football team by joining as a kicker.

Although the coach, who believes in traditional football, is hardly thrilled to have a girl try out, he puts her on the team because she's has talent as a kicker. With her help, the football team squeaks through the first few games. Brandon, who is the team manager, realizes that they will need to think creatively and devise unusual plays if they want to go all the way to the championships. To Brandon's surprise, he convinces Coach Knox to let the team "have more fun."

Soon they are playing a crazy game of football that takes their opponents by surprise, and they are winning game after game. While this is happening, Sarah becomes the romantic target of one of her teammates, and Brandon makes a special friend of a cheerleader named Janice.

On the way to the tournament, all the major characters learn a lot about having fun, making friends, and not pigeonholing girls in the world of sports.

Discussion Starters and Multidisciplinary Activities

1 Coach Knox's leadership style regarding football plays changes from being like that of a marine drill sergeant to being like that of a creative clown. Ask students to discuss for each leadership style why the football players in the story complained or worried while playing for Coach Knox.

2 When Brandon feels too much stress from his duties as the football team manager, he releases tension by shooting baskets. Allow time for students to discuss what they like to do to relieve stress.

3 When the story ends, what will happen during the basketball season is left for the reader to imagine. Have students discuss whether they think Janice will try out for the team and if they think she will make the team.

4 Other than the cover illustration, there are no illustrations for this book. Encourage students to supply illustrations for key events of the story. They may use any medium they prefer and should note the page of the book where they would include the illustration. Display the illustrations in the classroom.

5 Have pairs of interested students study the sports section of a local newspaper and then write newspaper-style sports accounts of the championship game in the story. Have the students share their accounts with the class. For each account, ask the class if the "reporter" succeeded in capturing the style of a newspaper sports writer.

6 Warm-ups are important to Coach Knox. Ask the physical education teacher to discuss the importance of warming up before any major physical exertion. Students might take turns leading the class through the warm-ups before a physical education class.

📖 *Matt's Crusade*

by Margot Marek
New York: Alfred A. Knopf, 1988. 148p.

FICTION

This book will appeal to fourth and fifth graders. The central character, Matt Tyson, is a seventh-grader. The book is not illustrated.

Matt dreams of being on the junior high football team as a seventh-grader. His dad, a Vietnam War veteran with an artificial leg, was once a great football player. He helps Matt train by throwing him passes and encouraging him.

Matt tries out for the team along with his best friend, Paul, and they do well enough to make the team. Although they aren't in the starting lineup, the coach gives them some playing time. Matt does better than Paul, who is especially nervous when his friend isn't there to catch passes.

A new social studies teacher, Mr. Behringer, is leading a protest against a nearby installation of nuclear missiles. The teacher has a daughter, Allie, who becomes Matt's partner for writing a report.

As Matt talks with Allie, he finds that he would like to join the political activists in their protest but knows that his father and his father's veteran friends would not approve. Also, the protest march is scheduled on a football Saturday.

Matt joins the protest. When trouble breaks out, he gets caught by one of the soldiers while helping Allie escape. Matt is taken to jail, bailed out by his father, and comes home to a celebration with family and friends.

Discussion Starters and Multidisciplinary Activities

1. Ask students to discuss how the topic of Matt and Allie's social studies report, "The Children's Crusade," relates to the central theme of the story.

2. On the camping trip, Paul and Matt are tipped out of the boat into the river. The boys get angry at one another. Have students discuss this incident. What does it show about Matt, his father, and his friend Paul?

3. Matt's mother is an interesting character; she finds it difficult to side with either her husband or her son. Ask students to discuss whether they think her views are more similar to Matt's or her husband's views. Have students quote passages from the book to support their opinions.

4. Invite a group of four or six students to present a panel discussion to the class. Half the panel should support and the other half oppose the missile site proposed in this story. Ask students to research missiles and missile sites before they present their positions.

5. There are no illustrations for this book except for the cover illustration. Invite students, using media of their choice, to make an illustration for the book, noting the page of the book where they would include the illustration. Post the illustrations on a classroom bulletin board.

6. Demonstrate propulsion for the class: Thread a length of fishing line through a plastic straw. Have two students each hold a dowel and stand 6 feet apart. Fasten the ends of the line to the dowels. Make a hole in the cap of an empty shampoo bottle. With the cap removed, pour 1 inch of vinegar into the bottle and then tape it to the straw (lay the bottle horizontally and position it at one end of the fishing line, with the open end of the bottle to the dowel). Put 3 teaspoons of baking soda into a tissue and poke the tissue into the bottle. Screw on the cap, shake the bottle back and forth, and let go. As the vinegar and baking soda interact, the bottle will travel like a rocket.

From *Exploring the World of Sports.* © 1998 Phyllis J. Perry. Teacher Ideas Press. (800) 237-6124.

Bridges and Poetry

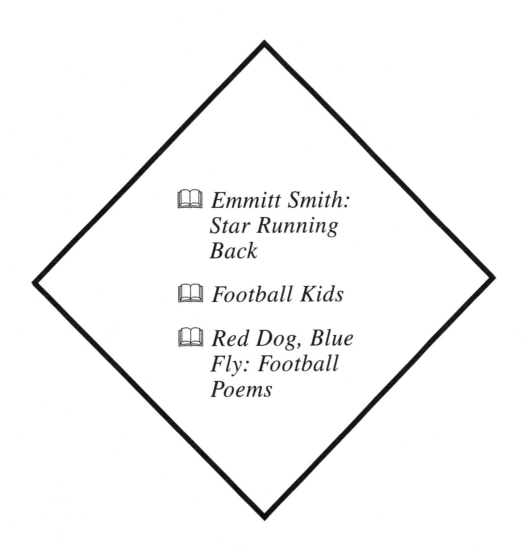

  📖 *Emmitt Smith: Star Running Back*

  📖 *Football Kids*

  📖 *Red Dog, Blue Fly: Football Poems*

 # Emmitt Smith: Star Running Back

BRIDGES AND POETRY

by Jeff Savage
Springfield, NJ: Enslow, 1996. 104p.

Part of a series featuring athletes, Sports Reports, this bridge book discusses in a story format what Emmitt Smith was like as a young child. His schooling and professional career are discussed as well. The book is illustrated with black-and-white photographs and will appeal to students in grades three through five.

As a young boy, Emmitt Smith followed five rules, which helped make him a superstar in the National Football League (NFL): Respect other people; respect your elders; go out and put a full effort into your job; go to school and learn something; don't go to school to play.

Emmitt was eight years old when he first played organized football. By the time he reached high school, he was experienced at playing quarterback and running back.

As a ninth-grader, he made the starting team as tailback. His sophomore year was even better, with seven 200-yard games and a win in the state championships. Letters began to arrive—many colleges sought to recruit him for their football teams.

Emmitt chose to go to the University of Florida and play for the Gators. He had a good first year but was injured in his second year. The following year, the university had problems with National Collegiate Athletic Association (NCAA) violations, and the entire coaching staff eventually resigned. Emmitt Smith decided to turn professional and was drafted by the Dallas Cowboys. He was named the NFL Rookie of the Year. He helped the Cowboys win two consecutive Super Bowls, in 1993 and 1994.

Possible Topics for Further Investigation

1   This book, published in 1996, invites interested students to write to Mr. Emmitt Smith, c/o Dallas Cowboys, One Cowboys Parkway, Irving, TX 75063. Have a pair of students write a letter to Emmitt Smith asking a question or two of interest and perhaps requesting an autographed picture. The students should include a self-addressed, stamped envelope that is at least 6 by 9 inches in size. They should carefully proofread the letter before sending it. If a response is received, have the students share it with the class.

2   Page 101 contains interesting statistics, including college and NFL rushing totals. Ask a small group of students to prepare a set of math story problems (including an answer key) using the numerical data provided on this page. Sample problems might include: Compare the total rushing yards for the Gators in 1987, 1988, and 1989 with the total rushing yards for the Cowboys in 1990, 1991, and 1992. Did Smith rush more yards during his 1987–1989 period of college football or during his 1990–1992 period of NFL football? What is the percentage of increase or decrease? Photocopy the story problems for the class to solve.

3   Emmitt Smith says that he's "chasing legends" and that he wants to be the all-time NFL rushing leader. Have students, with the help of a media specialist, research Smith's rushing career. How many yards has Smith rushed to date? What are the records held by Walter Payton, Tony Dorsett, Jim Brown, and Eric Dickerson? Have the students share their findings with the class.

 *Football Kids*

by George Sullivan
New York: Cobblehill Books, 1990. 96p.

**BRIDGES
AND POETRY**

This book will appeal to students in grades four through eight. It is based on interviews with seven high school football players. The text is illustrated with black-and-white photographs. The interviewed students emphasize that being on a football team demands a lot of time. Between homework and football practice, there is little free time.

The first of the seven players interviewed is Jared Dolce, who is a linebacker. He also punts and kicks. Jared explains that linebackers need to be big, fast, tough, and smart. Bruce Campbell and Charles Andruss both play quarterback. They point out that like generals, quarterbacks must be able to lead.

Jim Little is an offensive tackle. His job is to protect the quarterback and block for the runners. His position requires him to think quickly because he has different assignments for each play. Steve Kratis plays offensive and defensive tackle. On defense, he tries to sack the quarterback or stop the run.

Felix Valdez plays halfback and safety. His position on the team requires speed and natural running ability. One piece of advice that Felix gives young players is to learn to accept criticism and try to do better next time.

Mike Kelly plays split end and safety. His main job is that of pass receiver. He doubts that he has a future in football because he is neither big enough nor fast enough. He says that though football is fun, it's not his whole life.

Possible Topics for Further Investigation

1. In the interview with Jim Little, it becomes clear that the offensive tackle is one of the least recognized positions on the football team. This is partly because there are no statistics associated with the offensive tackle. There is no record for pass completions, yardage gained, percentage of attempted extra points scored, and so on for offensive tackles. To test how well-known this position is, have two students make up an optional football quiz for the class. Using names of players from teams in your area, the students should ask students to identify quarterbacks, pass receivers, kickers, and offensive and defensive tackles. Is one group of players more well-known than another? How well-known are the offensive tackles? This is a good opportunity to discuss teamwork. Without good blocking, many plays wouldn't work, but those who block don't get the recognition of quarterbacks and pass receivers. Are there other situations in which people who make significant contributions are not appreciated?

2. Some students in the class will be more familiar with football than others. Have two knowledgeable students make a chart of two football teams on the field. The chart should identify which side is playing defense and which side is playing offense, show where each player on each team might stand for a particular offensive strategy and defensive counterstrategy, and identify each player's position. The chart should also identify the particular offensive strategy shown (wishbone, etc.).

3. The author of this book also took the photographs that illustrate it. Encourage a pair of interested students to attend a local high school or middle school sporting event (baseball, volleyball, football, soccer, track and field, etc.) and take still and action photographs. Allow time for the students to share the photographs with the class and explain the type of camera and film that they used.

Red Dog, Blue Fly: Football Poems

by Sharon Bell Mathis
illustrated by Jan Spivey Gilchrist
New York: Viking, 1991. 32p. (unnumbered)

This book of poetry about football will appeal to students in all elementary grades. It is a large-format book with full-color illustrations on every page.

The first poem, "Red Dog, Blue Fly," is about remembering signals for the offense and defense in a football game. This is not an easy task for the boy in this poem. Signals make him tense and are a kind of boogeyman lullaby.

The second poem, "Football," depicts the ball as a brat who plays too hard and too rough. On the facing page, "Coach" spells out what to do on offense and defense. To the coach, it's simple as 1, 2, 3 and not complicated at all.

"Monster Man" describes sacking the quarterback. "Quarterback" describes how this key player can miss nothing and must see everything to fire the game forward.

"Touchdown" describes the thrill of scoring, "Ebonee" discusses a girl on the team, who does everything right as a running back, and "Leg Broken" describes the hopes and fears of parents of a young player who follows his dream and plays for the team but breaks a leg. "Cousins" describes how two boys square off on the playing field, each a major player on his team, but afterwards enjoy a pillow fight together at home.

Other poems include "Cheerleaders," "Playoff Pizza," "Championship," "Trophy," and "Victory Banquet."

Discussion Starters and Multidisciplinary Activities

1   After sharing the entire book of poems with the class, ask them to think of the collection as a story with a beginning, middle, and ending. Which poems belong to the beginning? The middle? The ending?

2   Sometimes, as in the poem "Cousins," relatives or friends find themselves competing. Ask students to describe events in their lives during which they found themselves in competition with good friends or relatives. What happened? How did they feel?

3   Have students tell which of the poems in this book is their favorite. Why?

4   At the victory banquet, team members stood at the microphone to speak. Invite students to role play victory banquet speeches, giving brief remarks as the quarterback, the player who broke his leg, and the girl who played running back.

5   The cheerleaders try to "jazz the crowd." Besides jumping, twirling, and using their pompons, the cheerleaders make up cheers that often incorporate the name of the school or the name of the school mascot. Have a pair of students make up an original cheer for your school and teach it to the class.

6   This team celebrates victory with a pizza party. Have the class discuss other kinds of victory parties. Have the class vote to determine their favorite type of party. Display the results on a simple graph, showing the kind of party along the horizontal axis and the number of students who voted for it along the vertical axis.

Football

 Nonfiction Connections

- 📖 *Barry Sanders: Rocket Running Back*
- 📖 *The Best Players: The Year in Sports 1994*
- 📖 *The First Book of Football*
- 📖 *Football*
- 📖 *Jerry Rice*
- 📖 *Joe Montana*
- 📖 *Joe Namath*
- 📖 *Steve Young: Star Quarterback*
- 📖 *The Super Book of Football*
- 📖 *Walter Payton*
- 📖 *William Perry: The Refrigerator*

📖 *Barry Sanders: Rocket Running Back*

NONFICTION CONNECTIONS

by Jack Kavanagh
Minneapolis, MN: Lerner, 1994. 56p.

This book will appeal to readers in grades three through five. It is illustrated with black-and-white photographs.

Born on July 16, 1968, Barry Sanders, one of eleven children, grew up in Wichita, Kansas. He played lots of sports with his brother, Bryan. Weighing less than 150 pounds, Barry Sanders was small for high school football. He did not make the starting lineup but caught passes as a wide receiver and ran back kicks. His brother, playing tailback, was a star ball carrier in high school and went to Northwestern University on a football scholarship.

Barry Sanders won a scholarship to Oklahoma State University, where he was assigned to special teams for punt and kickoff returns. He studied hard and lifted weights to increase his bulk and strength.

He led the National Collegiate Athletic Association (NCAA) in 1987 in kickoff returns and was second in the nation in punt returns.

In his junior year, Barry Sanders set a number of NCAA records and led the nation with 39 touchdowns. He also won the Heisman Trophy in 1988. He decided to turn professional and was drafted by the Detroit Lions in 1988. He signed an excellent contract and immediately gave 10 percent of his signing bonus to his Baptist church in Wichita.

In his first professional season, he was named Offensive Rookie of the Year. The following season, he won the National Football League (NFL) rushing title. In his third season, the Lions won their first playoff game in 35 years.

Possible Topics for Further Investigation

1 Among football players, Barry Sanders is unusual. In college, he worked toward a degree in business management, studying economics, accounting, and statistics. Have a small group of students interview by phone or letter professors from a nearby college or university to learn more about these three fields. In what sort of work do people with degrees in economics, accounting, and statistics usually engage? Have the students explain to the class what Sanders studied and how this might be helpful to a star football player. Discuss why it is important for professional sports players to have vocational skills other than playing ball.

2 Barry Sanders was interviewed for a magazine story published by *Boy's Life*. Have two students, with the help of a media specialist, use the *Readers' Guide to Periodical Literature* to locate this article. In what issue of which year did the article appear? Have the students locate the article in the collection of back issues at a local library or through interlibrary loan. Have the students share highlights of the article with the class.

3 One of Barry Sanders's teammates, Mike Utley, suffered a spinal cord injury during a football game; the injury left him paralyzed from the chest down. Invite two students to interview a local doctor about how paralysis can result from a spinal cord injury. Have the students use drawings to help explain to the class where the spinal cord is, how it can be injured, and why paralysis can result.

The Best Players: The Year in Sports 1994

by Bob Italia
Minneapolis, MN: Abdo & Daughters, 1994. 32p.

NONFICTION CONNECTIONS

This book, part of the Sports Reference Library, is appropriate for third- through fifth-grade readers. It is illustrated with color photographs.

After the football season ends, sports writers, league players, and coaches look at statistics and compare performances. Some players and coaches then receive special recognition and awards. This book explains the various awards.

The National Football League (NFL) Player of the Year award is given to one player in each conference who has contributed the most to his team's success. It was first presented in 1938. Since 1970, United Press International (UPI) has given two Player of the Year awards, one to the National Football Conference (NFC) and one to the American Football Conference (AFC).

UPI created the NFL Rookie of the Year award in 1955. Today, the NFL Player of the Year award, presented by *The Sporting News*, is a top honor. NFL players vote to determine the winner.

Recognition is given to the quarterbacks who are leading passers, leading rushers, leading receivers, and leading scorers. These awards all recognize offensive leaders.

Recognition is given to defensive leaders for team defense, sacks, and interceptions. Special teams receive awards for punters, kickers, kick returns, and punt returns.

The NFL Coach of the Year award, presented by *The Sporting News*, bases its selection on the votes of NFL coaches. Pro Bowl team players are selected by league players featuring the NFC vs. the AFC.

Possible Topics for Further Investigation

1   Invite students to design a football board game: Make a playing board from a canvas art panel or stiff cardboard based on the "Football Field" drawings shown on page 4. Have students make (or purchase for them) six small football figures as playing pieces and position them side by side on one goal line, facing the opposite end zone. Obtain flash cards (division, multiplication, addition, subtraction, or fractions) that show math problems on the front and answers on the back. Have the scorekeeper turn over the flash cards. The first student to say the correct answer moves down the field 5 yards. Students who give a wrong answer must move back 5 yards. The first student to enter the end zone wins the game, shuffles the cards, and becomes the scorekeeper for the next game.

2   There will most likely be a group of football fanatics in any given class. Invite this group to meet and predict who will be named to the various positions for the next Pro Bowl, AFC or NFC. Have them print out a list of the names and positions using a computer. When the next Pro Bowl team is selected, have the students compare their predictions with the men who are actually named to the Pro Bowl teams.

3   Football is played in all kinds of weather. Sometimes the weather is hard on players and fans alike. How bundled up should you be when you go to the next game? Have four students research to determine the most reliable weather forecaster for your area. Each student should follow a particular television or newspaper forecaster's predictions every day for two weeks, recording the forecasted and actual highs, lows, and precipitation. Have the students compare the results and share with the class who is the most reliable forecaster.

The First Book of Football

NONFICTION
CONNECTIONS

by John Madden
New York: Crown, 1988. 90p.

This book will appeal to fourth- and fifth-grade readers. It is divided into three parts and is illustrated with black-and-white diagrams and photographs.

Part One, "Throw, Catch, Chase, and Kick," contains two chapters. The author believes that there is a football position for everyone and that anyone can play. Madden suggests that kids should simply get together and play, remembering that teamwork is important. Madden also says that without proper equipment and supervision, touch tackle is the game to play.

Part Two, "The Pros and What They Do," explains basic terms and shows basic formations on the field using diagrams. Sketches help explain short, middle, and long patterns. From a discussion of such things

as running plays and the jobs of each team member, the reader learns what to do when playing and what to look for when watching a game from the stands or watching a televised game.

Part Three, "The Pro Game," discusses winning and losing, what you'll see and ways to watch, downs and distance, packages and plays, making it in the National Football League (NFL), and five ingredients of greatness. Topics covered include injuries; audible signals in huddles; the blitz; play diagrams; first downs; second, third, long-yardage downs; goal-line plays; growth spurts; making your own luck; dealing with pressure; qualities that make for greatness; and other ways to stay in football besides playing.

Possible Topics for Further Investigation

1 On page 59 of this book is a photograph of Hall of Fame cornerback Willie Brown. Invite two students to research the Football Hall of Fame. They should answer the following questions (and other questions of interest) and share with the class what they learn. What is the Football Hall of Fame? In what year was it founded? How does a player become eligible for the Hall of Fame? Who chooses the players? Are there the same number of players inducted each year? What sort of ceremony is held to recognize induction into this group of players?

2 Research involves thinking like a detective. Invite two students to test their detective skills by finding information and recording the steps they take along the way. The author, John Madden, was one of two coaches to win 100 games during his first 10 years. Who was the other coach? Have the students take detailed notes of where they went for sources of information, what led them to the next step, and how and where they finally found the answer to this question. Have the students share their notes with the class to help other students develop their research skills.

3 Have a group of students design and make a football board game to be played by two teams of three players each. The game board should be shaped like a football field. A roll of the die determines who "has the ball" on the 20-yard line. Correctly answering questions on fact cards (math, history, etc.) allows players to advance. Incorrect answers result in "turnovers"—the other team gets the ball. Each touchdown scores 6 points. Bonus questions determine extra points after touchdowns (1 extra point can be scored after each touchdown). A timer may be set to indicate when the game is over.

Football

by Sue Boulais

Marco, FL: Bancroft-Sage, 1992. 48p.

This book is appropriate for third-through fifth-grade readers. It is illustrated with color photographs and contains a glossary. The author states that football can be played by people of many ages. The rules and requirements are modified from level to level.

An introductory chapter discusses the origins of the game of "futballe" and explains rugby football, soccer, and recent changes in the game Americans call football. Chapter One discusses football equipment, including the football, football uniform, helmet, mouthpiece, shoulder pads, rib and kidney pads, hip pads, thigh and knee pads, supporter, pants and jersey, and shoes.

Chapter Two explains the football field. Chapter Three explains the teams (offensive, defensive, and special teams) and their players and positions.

In Chapter Four, the reader learns about playing a football game, including passing, running, blocking, tackling, and kicking. Chapter Five explains how to go about learning such skills as centering, passing, receiving and running, blocking, tackling, and kicking. Chapter Six provides tips for getting and staying in shape such as exercising every day; eating and drinking properly; getting enough sleep; and not smoking, drinking, or using drugs.

The conclusion explains that football is a game of skill, strength, teamwork, and fun.

Possible Topics for Further Investigation

1 In televised football games, an oral running commentary explains various fouls and penalties for the viewer. For the spectator attending a game, this information is given audibly over a public address system, which can be difficult to hear over the crowd. The chart on page 29 of this book is useful for spectators, who might memorize it to help them better understand fouls and penalties when they attend games. Invite a few students to duplicate the six hand/arm signals from this page on tagboard and then explain to the class what each signal means. Post the drawings in the classroom.

2 The glossary of terms in this book offers useful definitions. Invite a group of students to use graph paper to prepare a football crossword puzzle (including an answer key), which contains words or terms from the glossary. Photocopy the puzzle for the class to solve. (Some computer programs are available to help make crossword puzzles. If students have access to such a program and have sufficient skills, they may enjoy creating their puzzle in this way.)

3 If appropriate to the age and skill level of students, have the physical education teacher, with the help of adult volunteers, take the class onto the school football field and provide instruction in passing and kicking to small groups. Though some students may be adept at these skills, others may never have thrown or kicked a football, so the emphasis should be on instruction and improvement, not perfection. Students will need help in learning how to hold, grip, throw, and follow through on a pass. They should learn the differences between place-kicking and punting and then practice each type of kick.

 *Jerry Rice*

by Rose Blue and Corinne Naden
New York: Chelsea House, 1995. 64p.

This book will interest third- through fifth-grade readers. It is part of the series Football Legends and is illustrated with black-and-white photographs.

Jerry Rice grew up in the small town of Crawford, Mississippi. He ran five miles to school each morning. During summers he helped his father, who was a brick mason. During his second year in high school, Jerry Rice began playing football.

Mississippi State wasn't interested in Jerry Rice, so he decided to attend Mississippi Valley State University, where he played for the Delta Devils. In his four years there, Jerry Rice set many records. He made 28 touchdowns in his senior year.

The San Francisco 49ers drafted Jerry Rice in the first round in 1985. He was paired with starting quarterback Joe Montana; together, they became one of the greatest quarterback-receiver combinations in the history of football. After a shaky first-season start, he was voted Rookie of the Year.

In 1989, the 49ers and Jerry Rice won Super Bowl XXIII, for which Rice received the Most Valuable Player award. The 49ers also won Super Bowl XXIV. In 1992, Jerry Rice, or Flash 80, as he was sometimes called, broke the all-time record for touchdown receptions when he scored his 101st touchdown. That same day, he surpassed 1,000 received yards in his career.

Possible Topics for Further Investigation

1 Flash 80, the nickname given to Jerry Rice, might be a good name for a comic-strip hero. Invite two students to collaborate on a week-long comic book adventure story. One might write and the other draw, or they might alternate writing and drawing. Have them develop an episode each day for five days and then post the strip on a classroom bulletin board. Flash 80 might be a football hero, or a hero in another setting. One of Flash 80's special powers should be his speed.

2 This book chronicles the remarkable career of Jerry Rice up to the beginning of the 1994 football season. Have a small group of students, with the help of a media specialist, research what has happened to Jerry Rice since then. Is he still playing? For what team? Has he set any new records beyond those listed on page 62 of the book? Has his team gone to any more Super Bowls? In an oral report, have the students share with the class what they learn.

3 Some athletes have been described as "poetry in motion." Jerry Rice is described as a player who seems to "glide" down the field; he is "elusive and tricky." Invite a group of students to write a short book of sports poetry. They might include long, narrative poems and short, lyrical poems, some that rhyme and others in free verse. Poems might be about any sport. Have students print using word processing software and, if desired, illustrate the poems (illustrations might be included on the poem pages or on separate pages) and then staple the pages together to make a book. Have students share the book of poetry with the class.

 *Joe Montana*

by Paul Wiener
New York: Chelsea House, 1995. 64p.

This book is appropriate for readers in grades four and five. It is part of a series of books, Football Legends, and is illustrated with black-and-white photographs.

Joe Montana was born in western Pennsylvania. He was an only child, and he loved playing with his father, who had taken part in sports in the navy. Like his father, he played football, basketball, and baseball. At age eight, he began playing quarterback for a peewee football team. He continued to play several sports in high school and was offered a football scholarship to attend Notre Dame.

As a freshman at Notre Dame, Joe Montana received little playing time. As a sophomore, he was the second-string quarterback. When the starting quarterback was injured, Montana took his place playing varsity ball. Then Montana suffered an injury and was out for the year. Notre Dame finished the 1977 season as the national collegiate football champions.

When he turned professional, Joe Montana was drafted by the San Francisco 49ers. Beginning in 1980, Montana shared the quarterback position with Steve DeBerg. After DeBerg was traded, Montana led the 49ers to victory in Super Bowl XVI. He won many honors before leaving the 49ers in 1993 to join the Kansas City Chiefs. Among his honors and records are three awards for Most Valuable Super Bowl Player, and holding the National Football League (NFL) record for the most seasons with more than 3,000 passing yards per season.

Possible Topics for Further Investigation

1   Sports figures are honored in many ways. The citizens of Ismay, a small town in Montana, renamed their town Joe in honor of Joe Montana. With permission of the principal, declare a "Sports Hero Day." Have a committee of students, working individually, ask students and teachers from fourth- and fifth-grade classes to list their favorite sports figures (men or women, from football, baseball, tennis, soccer, swimming, track and field, basketball, hockey, etc.). The committee members should pool the lists of names to determine the top 12 favorites for the ballot. Set up a polling booth at the school where interested students can "register" and vote for their favorite sports hero. (A local sporting goods store might be willing to contribute prizes for a drawing.) Announce the winner of the balloting and hold a celebration in honor of the hero and their particular sport.

2   Joe Montana was called the Comeback Kid. William Perry was called the Refrigerator. Have students make a deck of cards, half containing players' names and the other half the same players' nicknames. Use the deck to play the card game "SNAP." Deal out all the cards to two players. Put each stack face down. Take turns quickly turning over one card at a time. When there is a "match" (*William Perry* shows as the top card in one pile and *The Refrigerator* shows in the other pile), the first player to call "snap" takes all the cards beneath the matching card. The player with the most cards at the end of the game wins.

3   Sports figures are often employed to advertise products. Have students invent imaginary products and write a jingle or advertisement for the product featuring a sports figure. (William Perry might be a natural choice to advertise a new refrigerator.) Products such as toothpaste, cologne, sports cars, computers, or a line of clothing are possibilities. Allow time for students to "pitch" their products to the class.

 ## *Joe Namath*

by Bruce Chadwick
New York: Chelsea House, 1995. 64p.

**NONFICTION
CONNECTIONS**

This book, part of the series Football Legends, is appropriate for third- through fifth-graders. It is illustrated with black-and-white photographs.

Chapter 1 begins with a description of Super Bowl III in 1969. The American Football League (AFL) had played so poorly against the National Football League (NFL) teams during the previous two years that many people thought that the Super Bowl should be abandoned. Almost everyone thought that the New York Jets, an AFL team, would lose, perhaps by as much as 40 points. Under the quarterbacking of Joe Namath, though, the Jets won, 16-7.

Chapter 2 describes Namath's high school years, during which he played well in three sports. He was offered 52 college scholarships; he chose to attend the University of Alabama and play under Coach Bear Bryant.

In his sophomore year, Namath quarterbacked for the team. In his junior year, Coach Bryant suspended him for the remainder of the season for breaking training rules. Namath played a great senior year but developed problems with his knees.

Despite his knees, Namath was signed to the New York Jets and began his professional football career. Joe Namath got the name Broadway Joe because of his colorful night life and many girlfriends. In 1965, he was voted Rookie of the Year in the AFL. In 1968, *Sporting News* named him AFL Player of the Year. Throughout his professional career, his knees were a major problem. He missed two seasons but returned for another great year in 1972.

In 1977, Namath was released from the Jets; he then played a year at Los Angeles with the Rams. Joe Namath retired at the end of the 1977 season with many records.

Possible Topics for Further Investigation

1   Have a small group of students contact a local high school and obtain a copy of the year's football schedule (showing the dates, times, and opponents for the season). Using this information, have the students design and make a 12-by-18-inch poster to advertise the high school football team. If a color printer is available, students might design a color poster and make copies to hang in local schools.

2   Toward the end of each football season, fans get excited about the collegiate and professional bowl games. Have a group of interested students make for classroom display a scrapbook of the season's bowl games. There will be many newspaper and magazine articles predicting who will play in each bowl game, and there will be substantial coverage of each game. Have students cut out such articles and pictures for their scrapbook.

3   The Super Bowl has a long history. Encourage a pair of students to research the history of the Super Bowl and make a chart to display in the classroom. The chart should include the year, the teams that played, the coaches and quarterbacks, and the final score. They might also include highlights of the game. If students are reading *Joe Namath* during the fall or early winter—football season—they might want to predict which teams will go to the next Super Bowl and which team will win.

📖 *Steve Young: Star Quarterback*

by Ron Knapp
Springfield, NJ: Enslow, 1996. 104p.

This book is appropriate for third-through fifth-grade readers. It is part of a series, Sports Reports, and is illustrated with black-and-white photographs.

Steve Young attended Brigham Young University (BYU) in Provo, Utah. The University was named after his great-great-great grandfather, who led the Mormon settlers from New England to the Great Salt Lake. Steve Young's father, LeGrande Young, known as Grit, also attended BYU and was a star running back.

Steve Young hoped to be a starting quarterback for his college team, but he wasn't throwing the ball well. Still, he wasn't willing to switch to another position, so he kept practicing and improving. In his sophomore year, he was given a chance to be second-string quarterback on the team. In his junior year, he got the starting-quarterback position and was chosen the Western Athletic Conference (WAC) Offensive Player of the Year. In his senior year, he finished second in the Heisman Trophy balloting.

He started his professional career by playing in the United States Football League (USFL). After two years, he joined the Tampa Bay Buccaneers in the National Football League (NFL). He played for the Buccaneers for two seasons and then moved to the San Francisco 49ers. He was second-string quarterback to Joe Montana. After Montana was injured, Steve Young became the starting quarterback in 1995. In the 1995 Super Bowl, the 49ers beat the San Diego Chargers, 49-26.

Possible Topics for Further Investigation

1 This book discusses Mormonism and the Church of Jesus Christ of Latter-day Saints. It is estimated that there are 7 million Mormons in the world, most of whom live in the western United States. Invite a group of students to research Mormonism. What are the major tenets of this religion? Who was Brigham Young, and how was he involved in the Mormon Church? After reading this book, can the students identify how Mormonism influenced Steve Young's sports career? Have the students share with the class what they learn.

2 Because the Super Bowl has been in existence throughout their lifetime, students may not be aware that there wasn't always a Super Bowl. Invite a pair of students to research the history of the Super Bowl and to prepare a written report on this topic to share with the class. They should cite at least three sources of information in their bibliography.

3 Even though Steve Young has had a successful career in professional football, he also wants to become an attorney. Invite a local attorney to visit the class. Have students prepare questions to ask, which should be submitted to the attorney before the visit. Students might want to know where the attorney attended school, how long it took to get a law degree, in what field of law the attorney specializes, and what an attorney does. After the visit, have students write a thank you letter to the guest.

The Super Book of Football

by J. David Miller
Boston: Time Inc., 1990. 136p.

NONFICTION CONNECTIONS

This book will appeal to fourth- and fifth-grade readers. It is part of the Sports Illustrated for Kids series and is illustrated with black-and-white and color photographs. The book is divided into four sections, each containing two to four chapters.

Section I describes the origins of football, tracing the game from its beginnings in 1046 in England when boys kicked a skull, to the twelfth century when 100 players played on each team and played a violent game with almost no rules. Walter Camp is credited with being the father of American football. In 1880, he made the changes in rugby that brought the game closer to modern football. By 1890, Amos Alonzo Stagg had invented the formation that eventually became the standard T-formation. The modern era describes the origins of the National Football League (NFL), the American Football League (AFL), and the Super Bowl. Section II describes the various positions in football and discusses football strategy. Section III gives information about great moments and great players in the NFL, and discusses football legends.

Section IV, "Inside the NFL," contains a chapter on the American Football Conference (AFC), including the Western, Central, and Eastern divisions; a chapter on the National Football Conference (NFC), including the Western, Central, and Eastern divisions; and a chapter devoted to records, including Super Bowl results, Super Bowl Most Valuable Players, NFL and AFL champions, winning coaches, rushing and passing yardage, and more. A glossary of terms concludes the book.

Possible Topics for Further Investigation

1 Because this book was published in 1990, the section on records is now incomplete. Still, it provides a good starting point for students. Have a group of students, with the help of an interested adult or a media specialist, bring the records section of this book up-to-date by researching what has happened since Super Bowl XXIV. Have the students share their findings with the class.

2 Almost everyone has a favorite moment in football. Many such moments are highlighted in Chapter 6, "Great Moments in the NFL." Have pairs of students choose a favorite moment to role play. Students should rehearse—one student plays a reporter, the other a football star—and then tape-record the moment. The reporter should briefly outline what happened and why this was a great moment; the football star should describe how he contributed to the great moment and how it felt to be involved. (Background music might enhance the recording.) Have the students share the tape like a radio broadcast with the class.

3 In a foreword to this book, Herschel Walker expresses his concern about the lack of physical fitness in children ages 6 through 17. Invite a group of students to interview your school's physical education teacher. Possible questions to ask include: What is the President's Council on Physical Fitness? What special programs does the council sponsor? Does your school participate? What are the council's current statistics on physical fitness in children? Have the students share with the class what they learn.

📖 *Walter Payton*

by Philip Koslow
New York: Chelsea House, 1995. 64p.

This book will appeal to fourth- and fifth-grade readers. It is part of a series, Football Legends, and is illustrated with black-and-white photographs.

Walter Payton grew up in Mississippi. In his early years, he wasn't too interested in football. He seemed willing to let his older brother have the football honors while he devoted his time to playing drums and cymbals in the band. Persuaded to try out for the football team after his older brother, Eddie, had graduated, Payton agreed, with the understanding that he would continue to play in the band. He had a fine career as a halfback in high school and then played for Jackson State College, where he set an all-time collegiate scoring record, 46 points in a single game.

Payton joined the Chicago Bears in 1975; he was a first-round draft choice. During his 13-year career in the National Football League (NFL), he rushed for more than 1,000 yards in 10 seasons. He also set the single-game rushing record, 275 yards, and became the youngest player ever to win the Most Valuable Player award. In rushing, Payton gained 16,726 yards. In 1986, in Super Bowl XX, Payton and the Chicago Bears, known as the Monsters of the Midway, beat the New England Patriots, 46-10.

Payton retired from professional football in 1987. He was inducted into the Football Hall of Fame in 1993. For fun and to satisfy his competitive urges, he has taken up stock car racing.

Possible Topics for Further Investigation

1   This book discusses how, for a long period of time, the city of Chicago failed to produce championship teams. Baseball teams such as the Cubs and the White Sox, the Bears' football team, hockey's Black Hawks, and the Bulls' basketball team had some excellent players, but the teams didn't win championships. The author, Philip Koslow, feels that the rugged playing of some of these teams reflects the spirit of the city of Chicago as expressed by the poet Carl Sandburg in his "Chicago Poems." Invite a pair of students to locate this long poem by Sandburg, choose sections that they like, and read those sections to the class.

2   Sometimes football is played in snow and rain. Have students conduct a classroom experiment to show that if the temperature of water vapor decreases enough, the water vapor becomes liquid water: Fill a clean metal can half-full of warm water. Add 6 drops of green food coloring. When the water reaches room temperature, add ice cubes, one by one, to the water in the can. When the temperature of the water decreases enough, clear (not green) drops of water will form on the exterior of the can. The air outside the can contains water vapor. When the vapor touches the cold can, the temperature of the vapor decreases and it condenses into liquid water on the exterior of the can.

3   Following the life and games of a football player such as Walter Payton requires geography skills. Have students locate on a map of the United States the following places: Columbia, Mississippi; Kansas State University, Kansas; Jackson State College, Mississippi; New Orleans, Louisiana; Chicago, Illinois; Denver, Colorado; Detroit, Michigan; Kansas City, Kansas; Dallas, Texas; Tampa Bay, Florida; San Francisco, California; Miami, Florida; Canton, Ohio; and Lime Rock, Connecticut.

William Perry: The Refrigerator

by Andre Roberts
Chicago: Childrens Press, 1986. 45p.

This book will appeal to second- and third-grade readers. It is illustrated with black-and-white photographs and is part of a series, Sports Stars.

William Perry is an enormous man—he stood 6 feet 2 inches tall and weighed 358 pounds when he was drafted as a lineman for the Chicago Bears in 1985; he was a first-round choice. Many football fans thought that Coach Mike Ditka made a mistake in picking this big man.

All his life, William Perry has shown his natural ability as an athlete. As a young boy, he played peewee football. By eighth grade, he weighed 240 pounds. In high school, he played basketball and, in 1980, was named by *Parade* magazine to the All American Prep Team for basketball.

He chose to attend Clemson University in South Carolina, where he helped the football team win their first national championship in 1982 with a record of 11 wins, 0 losses. Perry set a conference record for sacking quarterbacks in his senior year, when he weighed 335 pounds.

When he joined the Chicago Bears in 1985, Perry didn't play much for the first few games. In the sixth game of the season against the San Francisco 49ers, he played both offense and defense. Sometimes he blocked and sometimes he ran with the ball.

In 1985, the Chicago Bears played in Super Bowl XX, and although he played mostly defense, William Perry also scored a touchdown. When he is not playing, Perry often spends time at his home in Aiken, South Carolina, where he enjoys fishing.

Possible Topics for Further Investigation

1. Ask a group of students to bring to class single-panel cartoons from newspapers and magazines. Discuss what makes a cartoon effective and then have students study the humorous picture of William Perry on page 39. Independently, have each student draw a "William Perry: The Refrigerator" cartoon. The intent of the cartoon might be to terrorize a team that is about to play the Chicago Bears, or to show what could happen to your weight if you raid the refrigerator too often. Post the cartoons on a classroom bulletin board.

2. William Perry was a big baby. He weighed 13 pounds 8 ounces at birth. Send home with each student a slip of paper requesting the parents to fill in the birth weight of the student. Use this data as the basis of a math lesson: What is the average weight at birth of the students in the class? What is the mean weight? Is there a difference between the average birth weight of males and the average birth weight of females? What is the difference between the heaviest and the lightest birth weight?

3. Although William Perry is a huge man, when he started football, he could run the 40-yard dash in 5.36 seconds. With the help of the physical education teacher, have interested students run a timed 40-yard dash. How does the fastest runner's time compare with William Perry's time? Although William Perry made a touchdown in 1985 during the Super Bowl, his major contributions were as a defensive player. Have students discuss why defense is so important in a football game.

Part IV
Soccer, Swimming, Track and Field

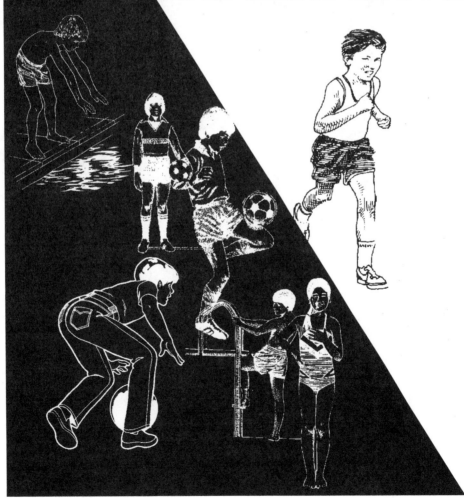

Soccer, Swimming, Track and Field

● FICTION ●

- 📖 *Albie the Lifeguard*
- 📖 *Cat Running*
- 📖 *The Detective Stars and the Case of the Super Soccer Team*
- 📖 *The End of the Race*
- 📖 *Going the Distance*

- 📖 *Joe's Pool*
- 📖 *The King of Hearts' Heart*
- 📖 *Let's Go Swimming!*
- 📖 *Soccer at Sandford*
- 📖 *When the Water Closes over My Head*
- 📖 *The Winning Stroke*

◆ BRIDGES AND POETRY ◆

- 📖 *Jesse Owens: Champion Athlete*
- 📖 *Total Soccer*
- 📖 *Sports Pages*

■ NONFICTION CONNECTIONS ■

- 📖 *Jackie Joyner-Kersee: Superwoman*
- 📖 *Know Your Game: Soccer*
- 📖 *Soccer*
- 📖 *Soccer Techniques in Pictures*
- 📖 *Swimming*
- 📖 *Swimming*
- 📖 *Swimming and Scuba Diving*

- 📖 *Synchronized Swimming Is for Me*
- 📖 *Track's Magnificent Milers*
- 📖 *Wilma Unlimited: How Wilma Randolph Became the World's Fastest Woman*
- 📖 *The Young Track and Field Athlete*

—OTHER TOPICS TO EXPLORE—

—discus throw	—high jump	—Pele	—scuba diving
—ear plugs	—javelin throw	—platform diving	—*Soccer* magazine
—goalie	—marathon	—relay teams	—triathlon

From *Exploring the World of Sports*. © 1998 Phyllis J. Perry. Teacher Ideas Press. (800) 237-6124.

● *Fiction* ●

- 📖 *Albie the Lifeguard*
- 📖 *Cat Running*
- 📖 *The Detective Stars and the Case of the Super Soccer Team*
- 📖 *The End of the Race*
- 📖 *Going the Distance*
- 📖 *Joe's Pool*
- 📖 *The King of Hearts' Heart*
- 📖 *Let's Go Swimming!*
- 📖 *Soccer at Sandford*
- 📖 *When the Water Closes over My Head*
- 📖 *The Winning Stroke*

Albie the Lifeguard

FICTION

by Louise Borden
illustrated by Elizabeth Sayles
New York: Scholastic, 1993. 32p. (unnumbered)

This picture book, illustrated with soft-colored pastel drawings, will appeal to kindergartners and first-grade students.

The story begins on the day the town pool opens for the summer. Ward, Will, Em, and Tony register for the Dolphin swim team. Albie does not register because he is sure that he cannot swim the length of the pool without stopping. Still, Albie has fun in the pool: He does a cannonball off the board; he dives for pennies at the bottom of the pool; he leaps into the deep end; and he sits underwater in the shallow end with his sisters.

Albie also watches and listens to the lifeguard. He decides that he will play lifeguard in his backyard. The next day, when his friends go to swim-team practice, Albie drags an old chair from the attic out to the wading pool in the yard. He climbs up into it, swings a whistle around his finger, and plays lifeguard. He pretends to rescue people and to work in the snack bar.

When swim practice is over each day, Albie hops on his bike and pedals to the town pool to play with his friends. He attends their swimming meets to cheer them to victory. In July, Albie registers for the team. He shows up for practice in a snazzy team suit, goggles, and a sleek cap. He practices the breaststroke, butterfly, backstroke, and freestyle. Every morning Albie arrives early; for a few minutes, he has the town pool all to himself.

Discussion Starters and Multidisciplinary Activities

1 Albie amuses himself happily throughout June, and doesn't register for the swim team until July. Have students discuss what they think might have happened if Albie's friends had urged him to register earlier than he did.

2 Albie pretends to solve lots of problems as a backyard lifeguard. Have students discuss other imaginary things that might have happened in Albie's pool.

3 Ask students to discuss why they think Albie arrives at the town pool before the rest of the swim team every morning.

4 Invite a lifeguard from a local pool to visit the class and discuss pool safety. Have one or more students follow up the visit with a thank you letter to the guest speaker.

5 Students may have experienced that it is easier to float in salt water than in fresh water. Have a student perform an experiment for the class: Fill a bowl with enough water to cover a fresh egg. Gently drop an egg into the water. It will sink because the liquids in the egg are more dense than the water. Carefully stir salt into the water. When enough salt has dissolved in the water (about 4 tablespoons of salt for every 1½ cups of water), the egg will rise. This happens because salt water is more dense than the liquids in the egg.

6 Public, motel, and hotel pools and hot tubs often display posters with safety rules. Invite students to make a list of pool rules that they think are important to follow at a public pool. Their list of rules might include pictures.

 *Cat Running*

 FICTION

by Zilpha Keatley Snyder
New York: Delacorte Press, 1994. 168p.

This story, told from the point of view of eleven-year-old Cat Kinsey, will appeal to fourth- and fifth-grade readers. It is set in California in the early 1930s.

Cat's father and the two children from her father's first marriage all work in the Kinseys' mercantile store. Cat thinks that her father is stingy and doesn't love her. Cat's mother is weak, never stands up to her husband, and suffers from terrible headaches that force her to rest most of the day.

Cat hopes to win the sixth-grade Play Day foot race at Brownwood School, but when her father won't permit her to wear slacks, she refuses to run. Instead of training for the race, Cat spends time exploring along a creek and finds a natural rock grotto. She brings things from home, including a special doll, and turns this spot into a secret retreat.

On Play Day, Zane Perkins, a barefoot boy from the Oakie camp, wins the big race. In the days that follow, Cat comes to know the Perkins family, especially five-year-old Samantha, who finds the grotto and plays there with Cat's doll. Cat is angry about this at first, but as she talks with members of the Perkins family, she grows in understanding and comes to love the little girl.

The crops have been picked and the migrant workers are about to leave. Cat goes to say good-bye to the Perkins and finds Samantha near death with pneumonia. When she runs five miles home to summon the doctor, Cat is credited with saving Samantha's life.

Discussion Starters and Multidisciplinary Activities

1 Ask students if they thought Cat would be teased into running the race on Play Day. What convinced them that she would or would not run? Did anyone expect Zane to win? Why?

2 Cat's brother finally tells her that the store is near bankruptcy and explains why their father seems so stingy. Cat feels better knowing the truth and thinks she should share this information with her mother, but she doesn't. Ask students to discuss whether they think Cat should have told her mother about the hard times at the store.

3 Have students discuss the character Janet. Was she a good friend to Cat? Would students like to have Janet for a friend? Why?

4 Invite a lawyer to visit the class and explain bankruptcy. What happens when a store goes bankrupt? Appoint a pair of students to be responsible for writing a follow-up thank you letter to the guest speaker.

5 Have a small group of students, with the help of a media specialist, research the winning times of various running events in the last summer Olympic Games. How fast were the entrants in the 100-yard dash, the relays, and the mile? Have the students list their findings on a chart and share it with the class.

6 Invite a group of students to research the Dust Bowl. What was it? What part of the country was involved? When were the Dust Bowl years? Could a Dust Bowl happen again? In an oral report, have the students share with the class what they learn.

The Detective Stars and the Case of the Super Soccer Team

 FICTION

by Caroline Levine
illustrated by Betsy Levine
New York: Cobblehill Books, 1994. 45p.

This short chapter book, illustrated with line drawings, will appeal to students in kindergarten through third grade.

Veronica and Ernest are "Detective Stars"—they have made a reputation by solving mysterious cases. In this story, they discover why a losing high school soccer team suddenly begins to win all their games. The coach of the Eagles is sure that the Foxes, a rival soccer team, are cheating. He gives the detectives two days to solve the case; otherwise, the Foxes will surely knock the Eagles out of contention for the championship cup.

Ernest and Veronica find that the members of the Foxes have taken ballet lessons. While watching a Foxes-Tigers game, the detectives notice that the Tigers are having trouble connecting with the ball. The detectives are suspicious of a substitute Foxes player who is wearing a big, thick jacket—on a hot day.

The detectives are convinced that the ballet lessons are a cover-up, and that the Foxes have some secret way of making goals. When Veronica notices how Ernest uses his remote-controlled car to give her a candy bar, she solves the case. Veronica dresses in an Eagle suit, with wings to conceal a remote control strapped to her arm. During the game, she points the remote control at the soccer ball, and the ball moves. The referee checks the ball and finds a motor in it, the controls of which are hidden under the coat of the Foxes substitute. The Eagles win when the Foxes forfeit the game.

Discussion Starters and Multidisciplinary Activities

1 The author explains that although Ernest is a little older than Veronica, Veronica is taller and more muscular. Have students discuss how Veronica's size and strength are used in the story. Are they important factors? Would these be important factors to players on a high school soccer team like the Eagles? Why?

2 Seeing Ernest use his remote-controlled car triggered an idea that helped Veronica solve the mystery. Ask students if they had other ideas about how they thought the Foxes were winning games. Discuss these ideas.

3 When people laughed at Veronica's Eagle costume, her face turned red in embarrassment. Ask students to discuss times when they wore unusual costumes. Did the costumes win them admiration, or did the costumes cause them embarrassment?

4 Have interested students consult with the art teacher and then construct an eagle costume. It might resemble the one in the book, or it might be a unique creation. Have the students share their costume with the class.

5 The illustrations in this book are similar to some used in newspaper and magazine cartoons. Have students collect cartoons for a week, bring them to class, and display them on a classroom bulletin board for discussion.

6 As a follow-up to activity 5 (above), have a few students create an original cartoon. It might be a political cartoon or a cartoon that deals with some humorous aspect of family or school life. In addition to the drawings, the cartoon should include captions or dialogue. Have students share their cartoons with the class.

From *Exploring the World of Sports.* © 1998 Phyllis J. Perry. Teacher Ideas Press. (800) 237-6124.

📖 *The End of the Race*

FICTION

by Dean Hughes

New York: Atheneum, 1993. 152p.

This book, a contemporary story set in Utah, will appeal to third- through fifth-grade readers.

Jared Olsen and Davin Carter have just finished sixth grade and are joining a summer track program. Both would like to run sprints, but both are assigned to run the 400-meter race for their track teams. The longer race is grueling, and they find it difficult to train, race, and then recover from pain and exhaustion after each race.

The boys begin to develop a rivalry, but a friendship, too. Their relationship is made more difficult by the fact that Davin is black and is always making racist comments. The boys learn that their fathers were friends in school but had a problem during their senior year that tore apart the friendship. Davin's father is bitter toward all whites and hates Jared's father.

The boys often ride their bikes together up a mountain. One day, Jared becomes so angry from Davin's racial taunts that he causes Davin to fall off his bike. When Jared realizes that Davin is injured, he bicycles to get help, pushing himself to the limits of endurance. The boys come through the experience as tentative friends.

Jared's father admits that he behaved badly during his senior year by allowing his black friend to be excluded from the big football party but says that he is sorry for his behavior and hopes that the two boys, in a more enlightened time, can do better than their fathers did and build a lasting friendship.

Discussion Starters and Multidisciplinary Activities

1. Jared finds himself uncomfortable with the racial comments Davin is always making, but he doesn't know what to say to stop him. Have students role play situations between Davin and Jared to help Jared find appropriate words to use to stop the racial put-downs.

2. Have students discuss the track coach. Do they think it likely that in an almost all-white community in Utah, the track coach would be black? What was the purpose of having a black coach in this story?

3. When the story ends, it seems likely that Davin and Jared will be friends. Have students discuss whether they think Davin's father and Jared's father will ever again be friends.

4. Have students clip pictures from newspapers and magazines and make a large collage of track and field events. Display the collage in the classroom.

5. When people think of track and field events, many think only of races. Have a pair of students research the track and field events held in the summer Olympics Games, make a complete list of the events, and share it with the class.

6. This story is set in the state of Utah. Ask a small number of interested students to learn more about the state. They might want to write to the Utah Travel Council, Council Hall/Capitol Hill, Salt Lake City, UT 84116, requesting information. They should be sure to do some research on the Great Salt Lake. They should share what they learn with the class.

Going the Distance

by Mary Jane Miller

New York: Viking, 1994. 151p.

This book will appeal to third- through fifth-grade readers. The central character, Loren Monroe, celebrates her 12th birthday during the course of the book.

Because Loren has an artist for a mother and a musician for a father, she has had to move with the family many times. Although she makes friends easily, Loren is tired of moving and always being the new kid. When her parents announce that they are going to Europe to see Loren's grandfather and to attend exhibits of her grandfather's and her mother's paintings, Loren is sad to leave Florida and her friend Stephanie. She moves to a suburb of Chicago to live with her grandmother, Nelia, who is a mystery writer.

A new family has just moved in next door to her grandmother. Loren quickly makes friends with the children, Ellie and her brother, RJ. Ellie and Loren try out and make the school swim team, the Dolphins. Loren wants to cut her hair because it's a problem when she swims, but Loren's long hair is important to her mother, who uses Loren as a model.

When Loren's mother returns, she explains that the family will be moving back to New York, and that Loren's grandfather will live with them. Loren will go to a boarding school so that when the artist family members are away, she'll have a place to stay.

Loren cuts her hair so that it won't interfere with her swimming and tries to explain what she needs from her family. In a compromise, Loren's family agrees to stay with Nelia until the end of the school year and then move to New York.

Discussion Starters and Multidisciplinary Activities

1   Have students discuss why they think swimming is so important to Loren.

2   Making new friends is difficult. Students may have faced this problem when they moved and changed schools. Allow time to discuss what students might do to help themselves make friends.

3   At the end of the story, Loren's mother says that Loren can choose whether she wants to model for her mother and her grandfather. Have students discuss what they think Loren will decide to do.

4   When Loren called her parents in Europe, the time in Europe was several hours later than the time in Chicago. Invite a small group of interested students to research time zones. Have them choose a variety of cities throughout the world and chart the hour and date for these cities when it is 8 A.M. on a specific day in your locale. Display the chart in the classroom.

5   Loren's mother became famous because of her painting "Loren by the Sea." With the help of an art educator, give students an opportunity to look at reprints of famous pictures that have a sea setting. Suggest that students do an original sea painting using media of their choice. Display the seascapes in the classroom.

6   Using the characters of the Dolphins coach, Ms. Lyndstrom, Loren, Ellie, Kaitlin, and Jenelle, have interested students write a chapter for the book in which the Dolphins meet the Racers in another swimming meet. What will be the outcome? Will Loren's grandparents and her mother and father attend the meet?

 *Joe's Pool*

FICTION

by Claire Henley
New York: Hyperion Books for Children, 1994. 28p. (unnumbered)

This simple picture book will appeal to readers in kindergarten through second grade. There are fewer than 100 words on each page, and the text is illustrated in bold colors.

Joe's Pool is a counting book. The story begins on a hot summer day. Joe has put on his bathing suit and is enjoying his brand-new wading pool, which is just perfect for one person. He lies back in the pool and sprinkles his toes with the watering can.

Then Jessica, a next-door neighbor, asks if she may join him. Joe agrees, thinking that there will be room in his pool for two. When Scruffy the dog dives in without being invited and shakes himself, Joe mumbles that the pool isn't big enough for three.

The counting format—adding more and more people to the pool—continues: A delivery man steps in and sprinkles himself; Joe's teacher cools her feet in the pool; the paperboy joins them; Joe's mother steps in to talk with his teacher; the mailwoman unties her shoes and climbs in; Mr. Fisher drops his groceries, hitches up his pants, and joins them; and the painter comes down his ladder and climbs into the pool.

Joe shouts that his pool isn't big enough for 10, but no one can hear him. He is angry and thinks of a plan to get rid of everybody. Before he does anything, though, the ice-cream man arrives, ringing his bell in the street. Everyone rushes out and, for a moment, Joe is left to himself. Then they all return and gather around the pool to have an ice-cream party. Joe sits alone in his pool, happily eating a Popsicle.

Discussion Starters and Multidisciplinary Activities

1   Several adults who normally would not go into a wading pool get into the pool in this story. Have students discuss which of these adults is least likely to go in a wading pool. Why?

2   Pets sometimes get into trouble around water. Dogs and cats may jump into swimming pools, or into lakes or oceans from boats, or they may jump into streams and ponds. Allow time for students to discuss their pets' escapades around water.

3   The ice-cream man has lots of treats. Ask students to draw and then share with the class a picture of the ice-cream treat they would most like to buy from an ice-cream vendor.

4   As a math problem, have students estimate and then determine how many quarts of water a large tub or a small pool can hold. This is a great outdoor activity for a hot day.

5   This story takes place on a hot summer day. To introduce students to simple graphing concepts, have them use a local newspaper for data and record the high temperature each day for one week, in degrees centigrade. Have them prepare a chart on tagboard. Along the vertical axis, mark degrees from 0 to 100. Along the horizontal axis, list the days of the week. Have students complete the chart to show the hottest and coolest days of the week.

6   Invite a student who has an aquarium to bring to class the special thermometer used to measure the temperature of the water. Using cool and warm tap water, have the student demonstrate how he or she checks the temperature of the fish tank.

The King of Hearts' Heart

by Sam Teague
Boston: Little, Brown, 1987. 186p.

Fourth- and fifth-grade readers will enjoy this book, written in the first person from the viewpoint of a seventh-grade boy named Harold.

Harold spends a lot of time with his neighbor, Billy. When the boys were four years old, they both fell from a tire swing. Harold was unhurt from the fall, but Billy sustained brain damage and now attends a special school.

Harold is trying hard to become good enough to run with the ninth-graders on the Lakeside Junior High track team. He is also trying to win the affections of a classmate, Kate Miller. Kate has a retarded brother, so she is particularly understanding of the friendship between Harold and Billy.

Harold practices, and Billy practices with him. On the day of tryouts, Harold wins his race and is jubilant. Unfortunately, though, Billy accidentally knocks him down and breaks Harold's arm, so Harold must quit the team for the season.

Billy, however, has a good chance to make the state trials and, eventually, go to the Special Olympic Games. Kate and Harold help Billy prepare for his event. By adding a weight to his right ankle, they help Billy fall less often.

He places second at the state trials and then goes to the Special Olympics. Although Billy doesn't win at the Olympics because another runner falls into him and knocks him down, he finishes the race. He is sad that he didn't win but happy that he has a friend like Harold, who gives him a special medal.

Discussion Starters and Multidisciplinary Activities

1 Billy doesn't win, but he finishes the race. Ask students to discuss the importance of winning versus the importance of competing and of challenging themselves.

2 When Billy makes so many new friends at the Special Olympic Games, his friend Harold gets angry for a brief time. Have students discuss why Harold is angry and how he overcomes his anger.

3 If students know children in the school with special needs, have them discuss how they interact with these students and the strengths these special-needs students have.

4 Billy has a chance to enter the Special Olympic Games. Ask a pair of interested students to research this topic. When did the Special Olympic Games begin? How often are the games held? Where are the games held?

5 Have students research the events held in the Special Olympic Games. Have people from your school district competed? Have the students share with the class what they learn.

6 Athletes are concerned about food energy. Have a student, with the help of an adult, perform the following demonstration for the class: Stick a needle into a nut; stick the other end of the needle into a cork so that it will stand upright on a table. Fill a Pyrex measuring cup with ¼ cup of cool tap water and measure its temperature. Burn the nut with a match until the nut is aflame. Hold the cup of water over the flame using tongs. When the nut stops burning, measure the temperature of the water. Nuts contain food energy (calories) in the form of oil. This energy, released as light and heat, raises the temperature of the water.

 *Let's Go Swimming!*

FICTION

by Shigeo Watanabe
illustrated by Yasuo Ohtomo
New York: Philomel, 1990. 32p. (unnumbered)

This picture book, with humorous pastel illustrations, will appeal to readers in kindergarten and first grade. Many animals are portrayed, with Bear being the central character.

The story begins on one of the hottest days that Bear can remember. It is too hot to read, ride a tricycle, or do anything else. Bear's mother comes up with the idea of filling a washtub in the yard with water from the garden hose.

Bear puts his toys in the washtub and plays happily. He sloshes the water to move around his duck, turtle, and boat as they float in the water. Using a sprinkling can, he makes it "rain" on his toys. Then Bear's mother gets the hose and sprinkles Bear with cold water.

Bear tries to swim in his tub, but it is too small. His chin and feet stick out over the edges. Mother suggests that Bear ask his father to take him to a swimming pool next Saturday.

On Saturday, Bear and his father take a bus to the pool. It is noisy because so many people are laughing and playing. In the dressing room, Bear and his father put on their suits and take showers. Bear cries in the cold shower and wants to go home.

When Bear and his father get near the pool, several of Bear's friends run up to tell him that swimming is fun. Bear stops crying and looks around: Everyone is having fun. Father takes Bear into the pool and holds him until he can float and swim. Once Bear is having fun, he asks if they can come again the next day.

Discussion Starters and Multidisciplinary Activities

1 After students have seen the pictures on the first 10 pages of the book (Bear is playing in his yard with the tub, which is clearly is not big enough for him to swim in), ask them if they can predict what might happen next.

2 Ask students to look at the two two-page picture spreads in the middle of the book. Have them identify the many kinds of animals that are swimming.

3 Invite students to tell swimming pool stories. Can any of the students float? Can any of the students swim? When and where did they learn? Did a relative or friend teach them?

4 Many people—children and adults—have sensitive skin. When they swim, they need sunscreen. Invite the school nurse to come to class and discuss why students need protection when they are in the sun for long periods of time.

5 Many animals are together in one pool in this book, but their natural habitats are quite different from one another. Have each student choose an animal from the story and, with the help of an adult volunteer, research its habitat. Have students share with the class what they learn.

6 If the animals in this story had played music while they were in the swimming pool, what sort of music might they have played? With the help of the school music teacher, have students listen to a variety of music and then choose a few pieces that they would play at the swimming pool. Have students discuss the music and try to explain why some piece would be appropriate.

📖 *Soccer at Sandford*

FICTION

by Rob Childs
London, England: Yearling Books, 1993. 192p.

This book will appeal to fourth- and fifth-graders who are interested in reading a book about playing soccer in England. It is illustrated with a few black-and-white sketches.

Another soccer season has begun at Sandford Primary School in England. A new teacher, Mr. Kenning, will coach the soccer team this year. Mr. Kenning encourages students interested in being footballers (soccer players) to register for the team, regardless of their year in school. He then holds trials and picks a team, a team captain, and substitutes.

For captain, Mr. Kenning selects Jeff Thompson, a good player with leadership ability who brings out the best in his teammates and who never gives up, even when it seems that the team might lose a game. One of the problematic players is Gary Clarke. Gary shows flashes of brilliance but often is in trouble at home and school and cannot be depended upon to show up for each game.

The Sandford team develops into a strong playing unit and has a chance to win the Frisborough Cup. They succeed in beating Kelworth and Fullerton in the first and second rounds, but they lose to Tanby. Now, even more important to the Sandford team than winning the cup is winning the league championship, which will give them another chance to play against Tanby.

The championship game is exciting, but some of Sandford's best players are out with injuries. In the final moments of the game, Jeff and Gary come through for their teammates.

Discussion Starters and Multidisciplinary Activities

1 The new coach makes a quick decision on who should be team captain, Jeff Thompson. Have students cite details from the text that support why they think Jeff was a good choice for this important position.

2 Invite students to discuss the way in which Mrs. Cowper handled Gary Clarke. When he was often absent or didn't pay attention to his schoolwork, she made him ineligible for soccer. Was this a just decision? Could she have handled it differently? How?

3 There are expressions in this book that will be new to students because the book was published in England. Ask students to discuss these expressions.

4 Page 167 shows a poster advertising a soccer match. Mr. Kenning noticed that a word in this poster was spelled incorrectly. Challenge students to make original posters advertising the match, with all words correctly spelled!

5 The author of this book, Rob Childs, is a teacher in Leicestershire, England. The book was typeset in Burley-in-Wharfedale, West Yorkshire. It was printed in Reading, Berkshire. Ask a pair of interested students to locate and then show the class these cities on a map of Great Britain.

6 World Championship Games held in soccer are detailed in magazines such as *Soccer*. Have a pair of students, with the help of a media specialist, locate a magazine describing soccer championships and share it with the class.

When the Water Closes over My Head

FICTION

by Donna Jo Napoli
illustrated by Nancy Poydar
New York: Dutton Children's Books, 1994. 132p.

This book will appeal to second- and third-grade readers. The central character is Mikey, who has just finished third grade. Each chapter has one black-and-white illustration.

Mikey is good at sports, particularly at pitching balls, but he cannot swim. He is dreading having to take swimming lessons again this summer. His sister, Victoria, is older and self-confident. His younger brother, Calvin, and his younger sister, Julie, aren't yet expected to be able to swim.

Mikey thinks that his brothers and sisters always get their own way and spoil things for him. Mikey makes a special picture for his father, and Calvin draws squiggles on it. Julie gives her ice cream to the family dog, and Mikey has to share his cone with her. Victoria always seems to be teasing him; she makes fun of his sandwiches because he puts olives in them.

Mikey's first day of swimming lessons goes badly. Because Mikey is hesitant, the instructor throws him in the water. Grandmother has a talk with Mikey before his second day of lessons. She tells him if he can work through that moment of fear when the water closes over his head, he'll be able to swim. She tells him to let her know when that happens because then she'll treat him to banana splits.

Mikey's next lesson goes well. He is even brave enough to help another girl in his class who gets cramps. Mikey can swim and is proud to tell his grandmother that it's "banana split time."

Discussion Starters and Multidisciplinary Activities

1. Encourage students to discuss the advantages and the disadvantages of having younger or older siblings. If a student is an only child, have that student tell whether he or she would prefer an older or a younger brother or sister and explain why.

2. Discuss what Victoria said and did that made Mikey mad. Still, in many ways, Victoria was a good older sister. Have students discuss the things she did that showed this.

3. Most of the book is about either traveling to the grandparents' home or learning to swim. Have students discuss why they think the author included the chapter "The Farm." What did this chapter contribute to the story?

4. Ask students to write an original short story in which a central character overcomes a fear of water and begins to enjoy spending time in the pool. Illustrations might be included.

5. Students have no doubt seen a list of pool rules. Ask students what is usually on a list of pool rules. Have them make a list of safety rules and explain why each rule is important.

6. There are many swimming strokes, including the freestyle, or the crawl; the breaststroke; and the butterfly. Have a pair of interested students research this topic and make simple diagrams to illustrate the swimming strokes. Have students label their diagrams and share them with the class by posting them on a classroom bulletin board.

The Winning Stroke

by Matt Christopher
illustrated by Karin Lidbeck
Boston: Little, Brown, 1994. 168p.

This book, illustrated with a few black-and-white sketches, will appeal to students in grades three through five. The central character, Jerry Grayson, is a middle school student.

Jerry loves baseball. It's the main thing in his life. During a baseball game, when sliding into second base, Jerry breaks his leg. After the cast has been removed, he undergoes therapy in a whirlpool. Bored with simply being in the whirlpool, Jerry agrees to accept an invitation to do some exercises in the school swimming pool.

Although he finishes most of his exercises before the swim team arrives, Jerry is intrigued and stays to watch the team swim.

One person on the swim team is Tanya Holman, a girl he has known since kindergarten, and she introduces him to other swimmers, including Tony.

Jerry realizes that he has becomes interested in swimming. He considers himself a good, competitive athlete, and he relates much of his baseball training to swimming on a team. Jerry practices a variety of strokes and finally is good enough to enter a meet.

After a slow start, Jerry becomes a competitive swimmer, willing to learn and to help his team whenever they need him. The action of the story culminates in a 200-yard medley relay race that Jerry helps his team win.

Discussion Starters and Multidisciplinary Activities

1   Some students may have sustained limb injuries that required a cast. Allow time for students to discuss their injuries and rehabilitation.

2   Jerry's parents are minor figures in the book, but they play a supportive role. Have students cite examples from the text that show how Jerry's parents support him in his recovery from the accident and in his newfound interest in swimming.

3   Have students discuss whether they think Jerry will eventually compete in both baseball and swimming or in only one sport. Have them justify their opinions.

4   A few black-and-white sketches illustrate this novel. Invite interested students to create an illustration for the book (noting the page where it might be included), using whatever medium they prefer. Have students share their illustrations with the class.

5   Maintaining a swimming pool is not as simple as one might think. Have a small group of interested students arrange to visit a pool and discuss pool maintenance with the pool owner or manager. They should take notes. Have the group give an oral presentation in class about the major factors involved in pool maintenance.

6   Swimmers practice many of their basic movements outside the water while standing up and counting. If there is a swimmer in the class, ask that student to demonstrate some of these exercises and explain what they are designed to accomplish.

◆ *Bridges and Poetry* ◆

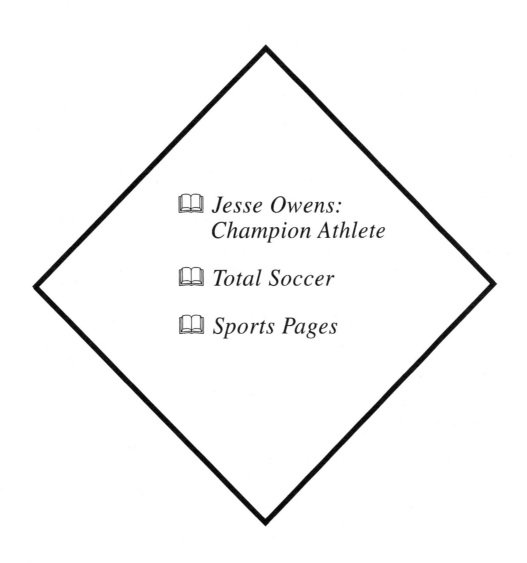

- 📖 *Jesse Owens: Champion Athlete*
- 📖 *Total Soccer*
- 📖 *Sports Pages*

**BRIDGES
AND POETRY**

📖 *Jesse Owens: Champion Athlete*

by Tony Gentry
New York: Chelsea House, 1990. 112p.

This bridge book, part of the Black Americans of Achievement series, is suitable for third- through fifth-grade readers. It is a biography of track great Jesse Owens, and is illustrated with black-and-white photographs.

J. C. Owens was born in Oakville, Alabama. His father was a sharecropper. When he was nine, the family moved to Cleveland. In Fairmont Junior High School, Jesse met Coach Charles Riley and began his career in running. Because of his part-time jobs, Jesse met his coach for practice early in the morning.

In his first year on the track team, Jesse broke world records for junior high school students. Jesse enrolled in East Technical High School. In 1933, at the National Interscholastic Meet in Chicago, Jesse tied the world record in the 100-yard dash and broke the world record in the 220-yard dash.

Jesse went to Ohio State University. In his sophomore year at the Big Ten Championships, he participated in the National Collegiate Track and Field Championship where he tied one world record and broke five others. During his junior year, he was suspended from the track team because of poor grades. He studied and continued to train. He qualified in three events at the Olympic trials.

In 1936, Germany hosted the summer Olympic Games (Adolph Hitler was chancellor of Germany at that time). On the first day of the games, Jesse Owens set an unofficial world record in the 100-meter run. Before the games were over, Jesse Owens had won four gold medals and set a new Olympic record in the broad jump.

Possible Topics for Further Investigation

1 This book describes how Adolph Hitler, believing in the superiority of white, non-Jewish, German athletes, thought that his country would dominate the 1936 summer Olympic Games. Have a small group of students, with the help of a media specialist, research the 1936 summer games. In which events did the Germans take medals? Why were the games not held in 1940 and 1944? Have the students present their findings to the class as a panel discussion.

2 One of the themes throughout this book is the effect of the Great Depression on Jesse Owens and his family. Have a group of students, with the help of a media specialist, research the Great Depression. Have them locate magazines, books, and articles about the Great Depression and write a short script for a filmstrip or video presentation. They should include photographs and drawings (have students ask the media specialist about permission requirements). Their narration of the script might be recorded against an appropriate musical background. Have the students present their piece to the class.

3 After winning his gold medals, Jesse Owens had a difficult time making a living. For example, he raced baseball players and horses, was a band conductor, campaigned for president, organized a basketball team, and managed a dry-cleaning company and a national physical fitness organization. Have a group of interested students make 9-by-12-inch illustrations depicting incidents in Jesse Owens's life after the 1936 Olympic Games. Arrange the drawings in chronological order on a classroom bulletin board.

📖 *Total Soccer*

by Dean Hughes
New York: Alfred A. Knopf, 1992. 101p.

This book will appeal to third- through fifth-grade readers. It serves as a bridge book because the author includes soccer strategies and practical, factual information after the story. There is one black-and-white illustration in each chapter.

The story begins with the Angel Park soccer team easily defeating the Desert Palm team. Some of the Angel Park team members, including Jacob and Heidi, are uncomfortable with the poor sportsmanship some of their fellow players showed. An English boy named Clayton is particularly arrogant.

Clayton plays spectacular soccer in the next game but hogs all the action. At half time, the coach reminds everyone that they are a *team*. Clayton doesn't get the message, though, so the coach takes him out of the game. The opponents tie the score. Clayton comes back in and makes two more goals, winning the game.

In their next game, against the Springers, Clayton again isn't a team player. The coach finally takes him out of the game. At half time, the score is 2-0, Springers. Clayton comes back in, cooperates, and Angel Park ties the score. Then Clayton becomes self-absorbed again and the Springers surge ahead to win.

After the game, Clayton is angry, and his teammates are mad at him. Jacob has a talk with Clayton at home, and Clayton confesses his worries about his father and going back to England. He changes his attitude, allowing the team to play "total" soccer, and Angel Park wins the championship game.

Possible Topics for Further Investigation

1 At the end of the story, the coach tells Clayton that he is very talented, so talented that he needn't worry about being able to play soccer back in England. The coach says, "You could even play in Brazil." Have a pair of students, with the help of a media specialist, research the game of soccer in Brazil. Is soccer a major sport there? Who are some of the most famous soccer players to have come out of Brazil? Was the coach paying Clayton a compliment? Have students share with the class what they learn.

2 Beginning on page 94, diagrams indicate particular strategies that a soccer team might use. Invite a coach or a soccer player to visit the class and talk about soccer. Provide the guest speaker with copies of the diagrams in the back of the book. Have the visitor explain the game of soccer and show on the chalkboard or an overhead projector how the strategies at the end of the book are designed to work. Have students send a follow-up letter to thank the guest speaker.

3 Every sport has a specialized vocabulary. If the class is spending several weeks exploring sports literature, a "vocabulary wall" might prove useful. Each time a student reads a sports book with specialized words, invite the student to add one or more words with brief definitions to a chart on the vocabulary wall. Separate charts might be used for baseball, basketball, football, soccer, swimming, and track and field.

 *Sports Pages*

**BRIDGES
AND POETRY**

by Arnold Adoff
illustrated by Steve Kuzma
New York: J. B. Lippincott, 1986. 79p.

This book of poetry includes 37 poems that celebrate a variety of sports. They will appeal to elementary students of all grade levels. The book is illustrated throughout with pencil sketches.

The first poem sets the tone for the book by suggesting, "I move from sport to sport as the seasons change, / as we change / and bend and grow. I learn. We learn." Students will find poems about many athletic activities.

Of particular interest to readers will be the poems on soccer, swimming, and track and field: "Watch Me on the Wing," "Prohibited Acts: Attacking from the Rear. Kicking. Tripping," "Though the Afternoon Was Freezing Cold," "Afternoons: Three," "Week Before a Monday Meet," "You," "Ground Bound," and "These Knees."

Students may also enjoy the poems about baseball, basketball, football, wrestling, skating, tennis, horseback riding, and general fitness. The poetry styles in this book may be new to students. The poems have uneven lines and spacing. The lines are formatted into various types of stanzas. Often, there is no regular rhyme scheme, although a careful reading will reveal the use of end and internal rhyme.

Discussion Starters and Multidisciplinary Activities

1. Have students read and discuss the message from the coach that begins the poem on page 24, "Coach Says: Listen Sonny." Does it sound realistic? Does it sound smart? How do students feel about the coach?

2. Page 61 contains a poem, "There Is a Very Ugly," which is about a girl with bruises and a charm bracelet. It concludes with the line "What a great time to be a girl." Ask students to discuss whether they think girls' sports and boys' sports get equal attention.

3. On page 42, "My Team Without Me" describes how painful it can be to sit out during a game. Ask students who have had this experience to describe how it felt.

4. The author of this book, Arnold Adoff, has written several other books and is the husband of another famous writer, Virginia Hamilton. Ask a small group of students to use the library catalog to find titles of other books these two authors have written and to share their list with the class.

5. Invite a trainer from a local gym to visit the class and discuss the importance of regular exercise and to describe the warm-ups, the exercise, and the cool-downs. Have students ask the trainer if different sports require different training and if he or she has any advice for elementary school athletes. Have students follow up the visit by writing a thank you letter to the guest.

6. Athletes preparing for a special event sometimes follow a particular diet for a few days. Such diets often include large amounts of carbohydrates. Ask the school cafeteria manager to visit the class and talk about the food groups and the importance of eating a variety of foods to help the body maintain peak condition, for non-athletes as well as athletes.

Soccer, Swimming, Track and Field

Nonfiction Connections

 *Jackie Joyner-Kersee: Superwoman*

by Margaret J. Goldstein and Jennifer Larson
Minneapolis, MN: Lerner, 1994. 56p.

NONFICTION CONNECTIONS

This book, divided into six chapters and illustrated with black-and-white photographs, is appropriate for third- through fifth-grade readers. The author begins the story of Jackie Joyner-Kersee at the 1992 summer Olympic Games in Barcelona, Spain, where she won the gold medal in the heptathlon after having also won the gold metal in the same event at the 1988 Olympic Games.

Jackie Joyner-Kersee grew up in East St. Louis. At age 15, Jackie won the Amateur Athletic Union (AAU) national junior pentathlon championship. She won this title four years in a row.

In high school, Jackie ran track and played basketball and volleyball. When she was a senior in high school, the U.S. Olympic Committee invited Jackie to try out for the Olympic long-jump team, but she didn't make the team. When she graduated in 1980, she accepted a basketball scholarship to the University of California at Los Angeles (UCLA).

After one semester at the university, Jackie's mother died, but Jackie continued with her schooling and her athletics. An assistant track coach who helped her train, Bob Kersee, eventually married Jackie. Bob Kersee convinced Jackie to train for the seven-part heptathlon, adding to her events the javelin throw and the 200-meter race.

In the 1984 summer Olympic Games, she won a silver medal in the heptathlon. In 1988, she won two gold medals and in 1992, she won another gold medal, all in the heptathlon. As founder of the Jackie Joyner-Kersee Community Foundation, she helps disadvantaged young people.

Possible Topics for Further Investigation

1 A group of students who read this book might want to trace Jackie Joyner-Kersee's travels. She was born and grew up in East St. Louis, Illinois. Her brother, Al Joyner, went to Arkansas State University. Jackie went to school at UCLA. In 1983, Jackie went to Helsinki, Finland, to take part in the Track and Field World Championships. In 1988, the Olympic trials were held in Indianapolis, and Jackie competed in the games in Seoul, South Korea. In the 1992 games, Jackie competed in Barcelona, Spain. In the 1996 games, she competed in Atlanta, Georgia. Have a pair of students point out to the class each of these cities using a world map.

2 Using the charts on page 54, which show Jackie Joyner-Kersee's heptathlon statistics, have a pair of students prepare math story problems (including an answer key) for the class to solve. Depending on skill level, these might include calculating the percentage of increase in her time in the 800-meter race between Seoul and Barcelona; converting the Seoul javelin throw from feet and inches into meters and centimeters; and so on.

3 Jackie Joyner-Kersee admired another UCLA track star, sprinter Evelyn Ashford, who won four Olympic gold medals. Have a pair of interested students, with the help of a media specialist, research in what years and in what events Evelyn Ashford won her gold medals. Where were the Olympic Games held in those years? Have the students share with the class what they learn.

📖 *Know Your Game: Soccer*

by Marc Bloom
New York: Scholastic, 1990. 64p.

**NONFICTION
CONNECTIONS**

This book, divided into 10 chapters, is appropriate for readers in grades three through five. It is illustrated with black-and-white drawings and is part of a series of books, Know Your Game.

In Chapter 1, the author writes about having fun. The author mentions that in the United States alone, there are an estimated 10 million people involved in soccer as players, coaches, and referees. Its popularity is at least partly related to the fact that soccer is a game that is fun to play.

Chapter 2 is devoted to soccer rules. The rules of soccer, sometimes called the "laws" of the game, involve every aspect of play. In Chapter 3, about soccer skills, the author discusses dribbling, passing, kicking, shooting, trapping, heading, tackling, and the throw-in. Chapter 4 stresses teamwork.

Chapter 5, about soccer gear, contains information about the soccer ball, shoes, shirts, shorts, socks, shin guards, and water bottles, as well as a special section devoted to goalies. Because soccer is a nonstop game, with no other break than half time, Chapter 6 discusses the importance of conditioning.

Chapter 7 discusses the organization of soccer and star soccer players. Chapter 8 emphasizes training rules. Chapter 9 explains the importance of good food and nutrition to soccer players. Chapter 10 discusses the importance of setting goals. The book concludes with a glossary of "Soccer Talk."

Possible Topics for Further Investigation

1 Have a small group of interested students research and share with the class information about the World Cup. This tournament for soccer is the equivalent of the World Series for baseball. More than 100 countries field national soccer teams. Only 24 teams qualify to attend the World Cup. In 1990, the United States earned a chance to play in the World Cup, qualifying for the first time in 40 years. Have students research what happened in the last World Cup. Where were the games played? How did the United States select players for its soccer team? When and where will the next World Cup be held?

2 Have students prepare a set of math story problems, based on facts in the book, for the class to solve. For example, if 10 million Americans are involved in soccer, what percentage of the U.S. population is involved? If only 24 of 113 countries are allowed to send a team to the World Cup, what percentage of teams go to the tournament? Have the students include an answer key.

3 In Chapter 7, about soccer organizations and star players, several soccer greats are mentioned: Pele, Kyle Rote Jr., Franz Beckenbauer, Giorgio Chinaglia, Shep Messing, Steve Zungul, Diego Maradona, and Todd Haskins. Knowledgeable students may want to add other names to the list. Invite a group of students to each choose one of these stars and find at least one other source of information about that player. In an oral report, have the students share with the class what they learn about the soccer star.

From *Exploring the World of Sports.* © 1998 Phyllis J. Perry. Teacher Ideas Press. (800) 237-6124.

Soccer

by Jane Mersky Leder
Marco, FL: Bancroft-Sage, 1992. 48p.

This book, which is part of the Learning How series, will appeal to students in grades three through five. Black-and-white diagrams and color photographs related to the game are included.

Chapter One presents a brief history of soccer and compares it to various other sports, such as hockey, basketball, and football. The game of soccer is explained, including information about the playing field, scoring, positions of various team members, and the cooperation and teamwork necessary for a soccer team to be successful.

Chapter Two explains the basic soccer skills, including kicking, passing, dribbling, trapping, and heading. Each of the skills is described, and photographs are used to clarify the text.

Chapter Three describes the action of an actual soccer game, such as the kickoff; the throw-in; the goal kick; the corner kick; and fouls and penalties, including the direct and indirect free kick. Also included is an explanation of the fact that the referee may decide not to call a foul, if calling the foul might inadvertently penalize the team that has been fouled. There is also a discussion of equipment, including shin guards, and a final admonition on the importance of being a good sport.

The book concludes with a discussion of the most famous of soccer players, Pele, and a brief recounting of his achievements and the role he played in popularizing the game in the United States. A three-page glossary of terms is included.

Possible Topics for Further Investigation

1 The book explains that the American Youth Soccer Organization (AYSO) has its own "Be a Good Sport" program. Have two interested students, with the help of a media specialist, research the AYSO. Students might research answers to the following questions: Is there an AYSO team in your town? How are members recruited for the team? What are the age requirements for play? Is there a state or national headquarters of the AYSO? Have the students write for a copy of free materials available about the program. They should include a 9-by-12-inch self-addressed, stamped envelope. Have the students share with the class what they learn.

2 Soccer is similar in some ways to football, rugby, basketball, and hockey, but the playing areas for these sports are different. Have a group of four students make a scale diagram of the playing areas for these four sports. They should include on the diagrams pertinent information about the playing area as it relates to the sport. For soccer, for example, the diagram should include the goal area, center circle, halfway line, 6-yard line, penalty area, and so on. Have the students post their diagrams in the classroom for students to see.

3 Invite a soccer player to visit the class and show and talk about the equipment used in a soccer game. The soccer ball, shin guards, and soccer shoes with soft cleats should be among the equipment displayed. Have students follow up the visit by writing a thank you note to the guest speaker.

Soccer Techniques in Pictures

by Michael Brown

New York: Perigee Books, 1991. 80p.

This book, part of the Sports Rules in Pictures series, will be helpful to young soccer players in all grades of elementary school. The book resembles the size and format of a magazine and is filled with black-and-white drawings.

When it comes to sports, most of us learn by doing. Reading about a topic is seldom sufficient. This book, however, provides easy-to-follow instructions that will help the reader master the game of soccer. This book focuses on techniques essential for all offensive and defensive positions to fully enjoy and play the game of soccer well.

The author explains that to be a good player, you must master the techniques on both your left and right sides. All good soccer players use their right and left feet and legs with equal ease. Because playing the game doesn't provide sufficient access to the ball to develop good techniques, practice sessions, following the directions in this book, are essential.

This book provides a number of expert tips, and it helps teach a player how to develop basic ball skills; take and maintain control of the ball during various game situations; build on goalkeeping drills; place the ball properly in front of a receiving player; develop defensive and offensive strategies; and put power behind a kick.

Also included is a glossary of terms and an order form for use in purchasing other Sports Rules in Pictures books.

Possible Topics for Further Investigation

1. Have a small group of student artists prepare a deck of playing cards for use in the classroom. This game, called "SOCKO SOCCER," is played like a traditional game of "SNAP." The cards should have either a matching picture or phrase, taken from the book. All the cards are dealt out to two or three players, who place the cards face down in a stack in front of them. The dealer is first, and the players take turns in clockwise order. In turn, each player quickly turns over a card from their stack. If there is a "match," (e.g., the phrase "a sole trap" and its matching picture), the player who first calls out "Socko!" takes all the other players' cards beneath the picture or drawing and adds them, face down, to the bottom of his or her stack. The winner is the player who has the most cards when the game ends.

2. Many magazines feature the sport of soccer, such as *Soccer Jr.* If back issues are available, have students make a collage using pictures cut from the old magazines. Display the collage on a classroom bulletin board.

3. Invite amateur photographers to take pictures at games and practice sessions and then prepare a 32-page picture book about soccer. The book might include close-ups of the ball; a shot of the playing field; a picture of the goalkeeper at the net; a picture of the game officials; and various action shots, such as a throw-in, trapping the ball with the foot, a kick using the outside of the foot, and players who are dribbling, heading, and so on. Have students mount the photos, bind the pages of the book, and include a brief text at the bottom of each page explaining what is happening in the picture. Have students share the book with the class.

📖 *Swimming*

by Jim Noble
New York: Bookwright, 1991. 32p.

This book will appeal to second- through fourth-grade readers. It is part of the Flying Start series and is illustrated with color drawings and photographs.

This book states that swimming is a basic skill, which when mastered, allows a person to take part in other exciting events such as racing, diving, swimming underwater, synchronized swimming, windsurfing, and even water polo.

The book gives details about swimming races, including the use of starting blocks, starting positions, the start signal, pads that record times by touch, the use of stopwatches, and the functions of judges.

The chapter "How to Begin" includes drawings that show how to push off and how to glide on your front and your back in a pool. It also explains the breaststroke, backstroke, and front crawl, and gives instruction on how to tread water.

The chapter "Getting In" explains various dives that can be performed in water that is at least 5 feet deep. These include the kneeling dive and the plunge dive. The use of an eyepiece is recommended for swimmers when water hurts their eyes.

The chapter "Flying Start Fitness" offers a few easy exercises for warm-ups. The final chapter of the book discusses the training that is necessary to be in peak form for an important race. Also included is a glossary of terms and a list of suggested books for additional reading.

Possible Topics for Further Investigation

1   Whether students are interested in swimming, some other sport, or just maintaining physical fitness, regular warm-up exercises are important. Ask the physical education teacher to spend part of a class period explaining and demonstrating how to do a number of exercises that would be appropriate to the age group of students in the class. Allow students to try these exercises under the guidance of the teacher.

2   This book states that in the 1988 Olympic Games, Adrian Moorhouse won the gold medal in the 100-meter breaststroke. Have an interested pair of students research swimming in the Olympic Games. Besides the breaststroke, what other swimming events are held? In the last Olympic Games, who won the gold, silver, and bronze medals in these events? What countries did the swimmers represent? Have students display in a chart the information they learn.

3   Two other sports that require swimming as a basic skill are mentioned in this book: windsurfing and water polo. Swimming is also an essential for those who enjoy sailing, surfboarding, and body surfing. Depending on where you live, these sports may or may not be well known to students. Have students, with the help of a media specialist, research these water sports. Many specialized magazines are published, such as *Sail*, *Motorboating and Sailing*, and *Windsurfing Magazine*. If such magazines are not available in the school or local library, they may be available through interlibrary loan. Have the students check out some of the recent issues of magazines and bring them to class to share with other students.

📖 *Swimming*

by Barry Wilner
illustrated by Art Seiden
Austin, TX: Raintree Steck-Vaughn, 1996. 48p.

This book is appropriate for students in grades three through five. It is illustrated with diagrams and color photographs. It is part of the How to Play the All-Star Way series.

Chapter 1 contains general information about swimming, including information about groups, federations, regions, and committees that run thousands of types of swim clubs.

Chapter 2 contains safety tips: Never swim alone; know the water; know yourself; protect yourself from the sun; and don't panic; with additional information on handling cramps, selecting swimming gear, and pool safety.

Chapters 3 through 8 discuss the freestyle, or crawl; the backstroke; the breaststroke; the butterfly stroke; race turning; and race diving. In each of these chapters are diagrams to help clarify the text.

Chapter 9 discusses swimming meets. After much training and practice, swim clubs and teams often schedule meets. To participate effectively, swimmers must prepare mentally; do warm-ups, including lots of stretching to loosen up; and understand the rules that will govern the meet.

The book concludes with names and addresses of U.S. Swimming Affiliates, including the Amateur Athletic Union of the U.S., Inc.; Disabled Sports, U.S.A.; and Sport for Understanding, which includes information on exchange programs for teenagers. Also included is a glossary and a list of suggested books for further reading.

Possible Topics for Further Investigation

1   This book shows several photographs of former Olympic gold medalists, including Mark Spitz, Eleanor Holm, Johnny Weismuller, Janet Evans, Nicole Haislett, and Don Shollander. Have a group of interested students research the history of swimmers from the United States in the Olympic Games. The researchers should learn in what year, in what country, and in what events U.S. swimmers have won gold medals. Have the students present their information in a chart for display in the classroom.

2   Page 24 has an insert on burning calories by swimming. Have a pair of interested students research how long it would take to burn 100 calories by engaging in sports or exercise. They might compare swimming, walking, running, skiing, and biking. Once the students have compiled their data, have them quiz the class. Class members must guess for how long they would need to swim, walk, run, and so forth to burn 100 calories. Generally, most students will underestimate how much exercise is needed to burn a particular number of calories.

3   Invite a qualified first-aid instructor to visit the class and discuss water safety. The instructor might discuss eating and swimming, cramps, sun protection, and safe behavior in and around a pool. Have the instructor demonstrate what to do if someone were to fall into the pool and be in danger of drowning. What should a trained person do? What should students do if they are good swimmers and come upon a person in trouble in the water? What can a non-swimmer do to help?

Swimming and Scuba Diving

by Michael Jay

New York: Warwick Press, 1990. 40p.

NONFICTION CONNECTIONS

The large-size format, diagrams, and colorful pictures in this book make it appealing to students in grades two through five.

The book begins with a discussion of basic strokes used in swimming: breast-stroke, front crawl, butterfly, and the butter-fly dolphin. For each of these strokes, the author presents practice tips and drawings to show a view of the stroke being used by a swimmer in the water.

The section on diving progresses from entering the water from a sitting position, to kneeling on one knee, to lunging, to a crouch, and finally to a plunge dive from the edge of the pool. This is followed by a presentation of a plain header dive.

The section "Voyage to Inner Space" begins with a discussion of inventions of early underwater divers, leading to the invention of the Aqua-Lung in 1942. This is followed by a section on using a mask, snorkel, and fins. In addition to describing this special equipment, there are instructions on finning and duck diving.

An equipment section describes dry suits and wet suits, life jackets, a weighted belt, and a wrist compass. Scuba (*s*elf-*c*ontained *u*nderwater *b*reathing *a*pparatus) divers depend on an underwater air supply. After pool training, Aqua-Lung students are usually assigned to a buddy and, with an instructor, make their first dive.

Final sections of the book discuss checks and dangers, talking underwater, surface marker buoys, exploring the seas, diving around the world, the living oceans, and sharks.

Possible Topics for Further Investigation

1. In the chapter "Voyage to Inner Space," several famous water explorers are discussed, including Edmund Halley, who devised a diving bell; John Lethridge and his diving machine; Augustus Siebe and his metal helmet and diving suit; and Emile Gagnon and Jacques Cousteau, who perfected the Aqua-Lung. Have a group of five students research these inventors and their contributions to underwater exploration. Each student should prepare a written report that includes a bibliography.

2. Some of the dangers faced even by experienced scuba divers are the bends (decompression sickness), the narcs (nitrogen narcosis), and loss of core temperature (hypothermia). Invite to class an experienced scuba diver who can discuss these health dangers, their signs and symptoms, and ways to avoid them. If possible, the scuba diver should bring an Aqua-Lung and describe its various parts to the students. Have a pair of students follow up the discussion with a thank you letter to the diver.

3. Perhaps by contacting a photography club or shop, you might be able to locate an underwater photographer who lives in your community and who would be willing to visit the class. If so, schedule a convenient time and date for this special event. Ask the photographer to bring a 35-millimeter camera or video camera that is typically used. Allow time for the visitor to present a short slide show of favorite underwater scenes captured on film and to discuss where and when the pictures were taken and what underwater sights they show.

📖 *Synchronized Swimming Is for Me*

by Susan Preston-Mauks
Minneapolis, MN: Lerner, 1983. 48p.

NONFICTION CONNECTIONS

This nonfiction book is presented from the viewpoint of Sara, whose favorite sport is synchronized swimming. It will appeal to students in grades three through five. Black-and-white photographs are used for illustration.

Synchronized swimming is defined as a sport that combines swimming skills with dancelike movements, choreographed and performed to music. Some of the basics are similar to dance and gymnastic techniques. The teacher of a synchronized swimming class teaches students to modify basic swimming strokes and kicks to help keep the body high above the water. Most important is sculling, in which hands and arms are used like oars. Propulsion sculls move the swimmer through the water headfirst or feetfirst.

Because synchronized swimming often requires swimmers to stay underwater for long periods of time, they must learn breath control. They also must practice underwater somersaults. The teacher explains how to do an eggbeater kick, which helps keep the upper part of the body well out of the water without sinking while the swimmer does a modified crawl stroke.

When students have mastered the basics, they are ready to learn one of hundreds of figures. The first one explained in this book is the tub. Explanations are also given for the ballet leg, the vertical position, the knight variation position, the crane position, the split position, and the bent-knee dolphin. Finally, the book discusses combining figures into a routine.

Possible Topics for Further Investigation

1. Buoyancy, the ability to float, is determined in humans by body build and lung capacity. Ask swimmers in the class to describe different floating positions that they have learned. Allow pairs of students to explore buoyancy by using shallow tubs of water to conduct the following experiments for the class: Gather a number of small items, such as nuts and bolts, a lemon, a hard-boiled egg, a tennis ball, a pencil, a piece of aluminum foil, a paper clip, the lid of a jar, a drinking straw, and so on. Have students first guess and then determine what floats and what sinks. Add a tablespoonful of salt to the water. Is there any difference in the buoyancy? Can the shape of a flat piece of foil be changed so that it sinks instead of floats? If a nail or nuts and bolts are placed on the lid of a jar, will they float? Have students discuss what they learn about sinking and floating.

2. Have a pair of students, with the help of a media specialist or an adult volunteer, research the Great Salt Lake. Where is it located? How "salty" is it? What makes this such a salty lake? Are there other salt lakes in the world? Have students share with the class what they learn.

3. In some parts of the world, salt is mined. Have students research and locate on a map the major salt deposits in the world. How is salt mined? When you buy a box of table salt, it may be marked "iodized." What does that mean? Of what importance is iodized salt? What is a goiter? Some people have salt restrictions in their diet, yet others take salt pills. Why? Have students share with the class what they learn about salt and the human body.

Track's Magnificent Milers

NONFICTION CONNECTIONS

by Nathan Aaseng
Minneapolis, MN: Lerner, 1981. 80p.

This book will be of interest to third-through fifth-grade readers. It is illustrated with black-and-white photographs. The author discusses some of history's greatest milers.

Glenn Cunningham grew up in Elkhart, Kansas. In 1934, he broke the world record for the mile by running it in 4:06.8.

Roger Bannister, born in Harlow, England, in 1929, became the first person to run a mile in under four minutes, 3:59.4, in 1954.

Herb Elliott, born in 1938 in Perth, Australia, set a world record of 3:35.6 in the 1,500-meter race in the 1960 summer Olympic Games, and had the two fastest mile races: 3:54.5 and 3:55.4.

Jim Ryun was born in Wichita, Kansas, in 1947. He became the first high school student to break the four-minute mile. In 1966, he set the world record for the mile: 3:51.3.

Hezekiah Kipchoge Keino, born in Kenya, Africa, won the mile event and set a world record of 3:34.9 in the 1968 summer Olympic Games.

Filbert Bayi of Karata, Tanzania, set a world record of 3:51.0 for the mile in 1975. Later that year, John Walker of New Zealand broke this record by running the mile in 3:49.4.

Sebastian Coe of Sheffield, England, set the world record for the mile in 1979 with a time of 3:49.0, and Steve Ovett of Brighton, England, in 1980 ran the mile in 3:48.8.

Mary Decker was born in Bunnvale, New Jersey, in 1958. In 1980, she broke three world records for women, a 4:17.55 mile, 1:59.7 in the 880-yard race, and 4:00.87 in the 1,500-meter race.

Possible Topics for Further Investigation

1 Track events are a good opportunity for introducing students to working with and making conversions from the metric system. Have a few students prepare for the class a worksheet on converting metric numbers. The worksheet might contain a conversion chart for students to use when answering such questions as: What fraction of a mile is 1,500 meters? How many meters are in a mile? How many feet are in a mile? Allow time in class for students to solve the problems.

2 Ten great milers are discussed in this book. Have a pair of students locate the hometowns of these 10 track greats and use pins and flags on a world map attached to a bulletin board to show where each of the great milers was born. The flags will show cities in Africa, Australia, England, Kansas, New Jersey, New Zealand, and Tanzania.

3 This book was published in 1981, and track records have changed since that time. Have a small group of students, with the help of a media specialist, research the current world-record holders for the 880-yard, 1,500-meter, and mile events. What are the times for the current records, for men and women? From what nations did the current world-record holders come? In an oral report, have the students share with the class what they learn.

Wilma Unlimited:
How Wilma Randolph Became
the World's Fastest Woman

**NONFICTION
CONNECTIONS**

by Kathleen Krull
illustrated by David Diaz
San Diego, CA: Harcourt Brace, 1996. 44p. (unnumbered)

This is a large-format picture book illustrated with simple and dramatic pictures. It will appeal to primary-grade students.

This book tells the story of a famous track and field athlete, Wilma Randolph. Wilma weighed just over 4 pounds at birth in Clarksville, Tennessee. No one knew if she would live, but Wilma had remarkable parents, and 19 older brothers and sisters to watch over her.

Although Wilma was small and sickly, she preferred running or jumping to walking. Just before she was five, Wilma got scarlet fever and polio. Her left leg twisted inward. Doctors and nurses showed Wilma exercises to help make her paralyzed leg stronger. She practiced these exercises at home.

When she was ready, she wore a heavy steel brace.

One Sunday at church, Wilma stayed outside instead of entering with the others. She removed her brace and slowly walked into the church. By age 12, she was no longer using the brace. In high school, Wilma played basketball and led her team to the state championships. A coach saw her play and helped her win a full athletic scholarship to Tennessee State University.

In 1960, Wilma Randolph arrived in Rome to represent the United States in the summer Olympic Games and won gold medals in the 100-meter dash, the 200-meter dash, and the 400-meter relay race.

Possible Topics for Further Investigation

1   Invite a small group of students to research infantile paralysis (polio), which was a dreaded disease during the 1940s. Before a cure was found in 1955, it had killed or crippled 357,000 Americans. Who found a cure for the disease? Have there been changes in the vaccine since that time? What is an iron lung, and how was it used for patients? Have students share with the class what they learn about infantile paralysis.

2   Primary-grade students may not find it easy to relate to large numbers and distances, such as 100, 200, and 400 meters. On the school playground, use a trundle wheel metric measuring device to mark off 100 meters. Working with the physical education teacher, have students participate in a 100-meter run. To avoid the pressure of having to win or lose, have students run in teams of four to six individuals. Note the starting time and the time for all team members to cross the finish line. Record the team time. Use this information to write math story problems for the class to solve. For example: What was the average time for students to run 100 meters?

3   Have a pair of students, with the help of a media specialist, research the track and field events that took place during the 1960 summer Olympic Games in Rome. What was the winning time in the women's 100-, 200-, and 400-meter relays? What were the winning times for women in those same events in the most recent summer Olympic Games? Have students share with the class what they learn.

From *Exploring the World of Sports*. © 1998 Phyllis J. Perry. Teacher Ideas Press. (800) 237-6124.

The Young Track and Field Athlete

by Colin Jackson
New York: Dorling Kindersley, 1996. 32p.

This book will appeal to students in grades three through five. It is illustrated with many full-color photographs featuring boys and girls.

The Young Track and Field Athlete is full of advice on how to improve in track and field events. It begins with a brief history, which notes that track and field is the oldest form of organized sport. A section on starting out describes appropriate gear and clothing, with an emphasis on shoes and cleats.

Two pages are devoted to exercises that will properly warm and stretch muscles. These warm-ups include neck exercises, arm circling, side bends, hamstring stretches, inner-thigh stretches, quadricep stretches, and calf stretches.

The most popular track and field events are sprints. Exercises called spring drills are detailed, including high knee lifts, heel flicks, and ankle rolls. There is an explanation of the use of starting blocks, which runners use in the 100-, 200-, and the 400-meter races.

Some track and field events are for middle and long distances, including the 800-meter, 1,500-meter, 3,000-meter, 5,000-meter, and 10,000-meter events. Various exercises are suggested for training or conditioning programs to help athletes build up stamina and muscle strength for these races.

Specific events included are the relay, hurdles, jumps, discus, javelin throw, shot put, decathlon, and heptathlon.

Possible Topics for Further Investigation

1. The introduction to this book was written by Gwen Torrence. Have a pair of interested students write a report about the life of this outstanding athlete. The students should include a bibliography that documents their sources of information. Where did she grow up and train? Who was her coach? In what Olympic Games did she participate? In what events did she participate? In an oral report, have the students share the highlights with the class.

2. Some shoes have cleats to provide a better grip on a track surface. These shoes are lighter than running shoes and provide less support. The cleats in these shoes are removable, and athletes carry a spare set and a wrench to use if a cleat is lost or damaged. Invite to class a track athlete who uses shoes with removable cleats. Have the athlete demonstrate to the class how these cleats can be removed and replaced. Have a student follow up the visit with a thank you note to the guest.

3. Some students will be familiar with metric equivalents (used in most countries of the world); others will be familiar only with the system of weights and measurements used in the United States. Have students prepare a demonstration of equivalents for the class, using scales, measuring tapes, charts, and other items. For example, the shot thrown in the shot put is 3.25 kilograms for girls, 4 kilograms for women, and 7.26 kilograms for men. What are the equivalents of these weights in pounds and ounces? The discus is thrown from a circle 2.5 meters in diameter. What is the equivalent of this distance in feet and inches?

Part V
Additional
Resources

📖 Fiction 📖

Baseball

Armstrong, Jennifer. *Patrick Doyle Is Full of Blarney*. New York: Random House, 1996.

Dygard, Thomas J. *Infield Hit*. New York: Morrow Junior Books, 1996.

Griffin, Geoffrey. *The Magic Bat*. Austin, TX: Raintree Steck-Vaughn, 1995.

Hall, Donald. *When Willard Met Babe Ruth*. San Diego, CA: Browndeer Press, 1996.

Lord, Bette Bao. *In the Year of the Boar and Jackie Robinson*. New York: Harper & Row Junior Books, 1984.

McConnachie, Brian. *Elmer and the Chickens vs. the Big League*. New York: Crown, 1992.

McCully, Emily Arnold. *Grandmas at Bat*. New York: HarperCollins, 1993.

Parrish, Peggy. *Play Ball, Amelia Bedelia*. New York: HarperCollins, 1996.

Patneaude, David. *The Last Man's Reward*. Morton Grove, IL: Whitman, 1996.

Prager, Annabelle. *The Baseball Birthday Party*. New York: Random House, 1995.

Spohn, David. *Home Field*. New York: Lothrop, Lee & Shepard, 1993.

Welch, Willy. *Playing Right Field*. New York: Scholastic, 1995.

Basketball

Barber, Barbara E. *Allie's Basketball Dream*. New York: Lee & Low Books, 1996.

Birdseye, Tom. *Tarantula Shoes*. New York: Holiday House, 1995.

Dygard, Thomas J. *Tournament Upstart*. New York: Morrow Junior Books, 1984.

Hughes, Dean. *Nothing but Net*. New York: Alfred A. Knopf, 1992.

——. *The Trophy*. New York: Alfred A. Knopf, 1994.

Maccarone, Grace. *The Gym Day Winner*. New York: Scholastic, 1996.

Marzollo, Jean. *Slam Dunk Saturday*. New York: Random House, 1994.

Myers, Walter Dean. *Hoop: A Novel*. New York: Delacorte Press, 1981.

Preller, James. *Space Jam*. New York: Scholastic, 1996.

Quattlebaum, Mary. *Jackson Jones and the Puddle of Thorns*. New York: Delacorte Press, 1994.

Soto, Gary. *Taking Sides*. San Diego, CA: Harcourt Brace Jovanovich, 1991.

Vecere, Joel. *A Story About Courage*. Austin, TX: Raintree Steck-Vaughn, 1992.

Football

Christopher, Matt. *Fighting Tackle*. Boston: Little, Brown, 1995.

———. *Tackle Without a Team*. Boston: Little, Brown, 1989.

———. *Undercover Tailback*. Boston: Little, Brown, 1992.

Delton, Judy. *Blue Skies, French Fries*. New York: Dell, 1988.

Friend, David. *Baseball, Football, Daddy, and Me*. New York: Viking, 1990.

Kessler, Leonard P. *Kick, Pass, and Run*. New York: HarperCollins, 1996.

Korman, Gordon. *The Zucchini Warriors*. New York: Scholastic, 1988.

Leggat, Bonnie-Alise. *Point, Pass & Point!* Kansas City, MO: Landmark Editions, 1992.

Marsh, Carole. *New York Silly Football Mysteries*. Vol. 1. Bath, NC: Gallopade, 1988.

Schwartz, Joel L. *Upchuck Summer's Revenge*. New York: Delacorte Press, 1990.

Twohill, Maggie. *Superbowl Upset*. New York: Bradbury Press, 1991.

Wunderli, Stephen. *The Heartbeat of Halftime*. New York: Henry Holt, 1996.

Soccer, Swimming, Track and Field

Bourgeois, Paulette. *Franklin Plays the Game*. New York: Scholastic, 1995.

Bridwell, Norman. *Clifford's Sports Day*. New York: Scholastic, 1996.

Brown, Susan M. *You're Dead, David Borelli*. New York: Atheneum Books for Young Readers, 1995.

Cleary, Beverly. *Strider*. New York: Morrow Junior Books, 1991.

Keene, Carolyn. *The Soccer Shoe Clue*. New York: Pocket Books, 1995.

Levy, Marilyn. *Run for Your Life*. Boston: Houghton Mifflin, 1996.

Naylor, Phyllis Reynolds. *Alice the Brave*. New York: Atheneum, 1995.

Rice, Eve. *Swim!* New York: Greenwillow Books, 1996.

Shreve, Susan Richard. *The Goalie*. New York: Tambourine Books, 1996.

Warner, Gertrude C. *The Mystery Cruise*. Morton Grove, IL: Whitman, 1992.

Weston, Martha. *Tuck in the Pool*. New York: Clarion Books, 1995.

Woolverton, Linda. *Running Before the Wind*. Boston: Houghton Mifflin, 1987.

📖 Nonfiction 📖

Baseball

Aaron, Hank, with Lonnie Wheeler. *I Had a Hammer: The Hank Aaron Story*. New York: HarperCollins, 1991.

Asche, Arthur T. *A Hard Road to Glory: A History of the African American Athlete*. Vol. 3. New York: Warner, 1988.

Aylesworth, Thomas G. *The Kids' World Almanac of Baseball*. New York: Pharos Books, 1993.

Brandt, Keith. *Babe Ruth: Home Run Hero*. Mahwah, NJ: Troll, 1986.

Charlton, James. *The Baseball Chronology*. New York: Macmillan, 1991.

Gutelle, Andrew. *Baseball's Best: Five True Stories*. New York: Random House, 1990.

Jaspersohn, William. *Bat, Ball, Glove: The Making of Major League Baseball Gear*. Boston: Little, Brown, 1989.

Kramer, Sydelle. *Baseball's Greatest Pitchers*. New York: Random House, 1992.

Obojski, Robert. *Baseball Bloopers & Other Curious Incidents*. New York: Sterling, 1989.

Torres, John Albert. *Sports Great Darryl Strawberry*. Hillside, NJ: Enslow, 1990.

Ward, Geoffrey C. *Who Invented the Game?* New York: Alfred A. Knopf, 1994.

Basketball

Aaseng, Nathan. *Basketball's Playmakers*. Minneapolis, MN: Lerner, 1983.

Anderson, Dave. *The Story of Basketball*. New York: Morrow Junior Books, 1988.

Bird, Larry, with Bob Ryan. *Bird: The Story of My Life*. New York: Doubleday, 1990.

Bloom, Marc. *Basketball*. New York: Scholastic, 1991.

Chamberlain, Wilt. *A View from Above*. New York: Penguin, 1991.

Frank, Steven. *Magic Johnson*. New York: Chelsea House, 1995.

George, Nelson. *Elevating the Game*. New York: HarperCollins, 1993.

Gutman, Bill. *Go for It: Basketball*. Lakeville, CT: Grey Castle Press, 1989.

Hollander, Zander, and Alex Sachare, eds. *The Official NBA Basketball Encyclopedia*. New York: Villard Books, 1989.

Nadel, Eric. *The Night Will Scored 100*. Dallas, TX: Taylor, 1990.

Ryan, Bob, and Dick Raphael. *The Boston Celtics*. New York: Addison-Wesley, 1989.

Shapiro, Miles. *Bill Russell: Basketball Great*. New York: Chelsea House, 1991.

Football

Aaseng, Nathan. *College Football's Hottest Rivalries*. Minneapolis, MN: Lerner, 1987.

Benagh, Jim. *Football: Startling Stories Behind the Records*. New York: Sterling, 1987.

Brenner, Richard J. *The Complete Super Bowl Story: Games I–XXIII*. Minneapolis, MN: Lerner, 1990.

Chadwick, Bruce. *Deion Sanders*. New York: Chelsea House, 1996.

———. *John Madden*. New York: Chelsea House, 1997.

Goodman, Michael E. *Green Bay Packers*. Mankato, MN: Creative Education, 1997.

Lamb, Kevin. *Portrait of Victory: Chicago Bears 1985*. Chicago: Bonus Books, 1986.

Lovett, Chip. *Miami Dolphins*. Mankato, MN: Creative Education, 1997.

Madden, John, and Dave Anderson. *One Knee Equals Two Feet (& Everything Else You Need to Know About Pro Football)*. New York: Villard Books, 1986.

Pierson, Don, and Jonathan Daniel. *The Super Season*. Chicago: Bonus Books, 1986.

Stanley, Loren. *San Diego Chargers*. Mankato, MN: Creative Education, 1997.

Whittingham, Richard. *Bears in Their Own Words*. Chicago: Contemporary Books, 1991.

Soccer, Swimming, Track and Field

Carson, Charles. *Make the Team: Swimming and Diving*. Boston: Little, Brown, 1991.

Coleman, Lori. *Fundamental Soccer*. Minneapolis, MN: Lerner, 1995.

Gutman, Bill. *Gail Devers*. Austin, TX: Raintree Steck-Vaughn, 1996.

Howard, Dale E. *Soccer Around the World*. Chicago: Childrens Press, 1994.

———. *Soccer Stars*. Chicago: Childrens Press, 1994.

Jensen, Julie. *Beginning Soccer*. Minneapolis, MN: Lerner, 1995.

Marx, Doug. *Track and Field*. Vero Beach, FL: Rourke, 1994.

Sandelson, Robert. *Swimming & Diving*. New York: Macmillan, 1991.

Sanford, William R. *Babe Dedrickson Zaharias*. New York: Crestwood House, 1993.

Schultz, Ron. *Looking Inside Sports Aerodynamics*. Santa Fe, NM: J. Muir, 1992.

📖 **Media** 📖

Allard, Harry. *Miss Nelson Has a Field Day*. Boston: Houghton Mifflin, 1989. 1 book, 1 audio cassette.

Christopher, Matt. *Baseball Pals*. Prince Frederick, MD: Recorded Books, 1996. 2 audio cassettes.

———. *The Dog That Pitched a No-Hitter*. Prince Frederick, MD: Recorded Books, 1996. 1 audio cassette.

———. *Tough to Tackle*. Old Greenwich, CT: Listening Library, 1995. 2 audio cassettes.

Cleary, Beverly. *Strider*. Prince Frederick, MD: Recorded Books, 1992. 2 audio cassettes.

Microsoft. *Explorapedia*. Redmond, WA: Microsoft, 1994. 2 discs. (Interactive CD-ROM encyclopedia for children.)

Sabin, Francene. *Jesse Owens: Olympic Hero*. Mahwah, NJ: Troll, 1986. 1 book, 1 audio cassette.

Sports Illustrated. *Multimedia Sports Almanac*. CD-ROM published by Star Press Multimedia, distributed by Softkey International, Inc., 1993.

Author, Title, Illustrator Index

About the Author

Phyllis J. Perry has worked as a teacher, an elementary school principal, a district curriculum specialist, a supervisor of student teachers, and as a director of talented and gifted education. She is the author of more than two dozen books for children and teachers including nine First Books for Franklin Watts and the Literature Bridges to Science series for Teacher Ideas Press.

Dr. Perry received her undergraduate degree from the University of California at Berkeley and her doctorate from the University of Colorado in Boulder. She now devotes full time to writing and lives with her husband, David, in Boulder, Colorado.

From Teacher Ideas Press

EXPLORING THE WORLD OF ANIMALS: Linking Fiction to Nonfiction
Phyllis J. Perry

Animals are a subject of intense fascination for young students. This book contains four sections—animals as pets, animals on the farm, animals in the woods, and animals in the wild. **Grades K–5.**
Literature Bridges to Science Series
xvii, 133p. 8½x11 paper ISBN 1-56308-517-8

RAINY, WINDY, SNOWY, SUNNY DAYS: Linking Fiction to Nonfiction
Phyllis J. Perry

Integrate language arts with science, social studies, and mathematics with summaries of children's literature and nonfiction books related to weather. **Grades K–5.**
Literature Bridges to Science Series
xiii, 147p. 8½x11 paper ISBN 1-56308-392-2

GUIDE TO MATH MATERIALS: Resources to Support the NCTM Standards
Phyllis J. Perry

Now you can easily locate the materials you need to implement the new NCTM math standards. Organized by such math topics as problem solving, estimation, and spatial relationships the book shows users where to find manipulatives and materials. **Grades K–4.**
xviii, 127p. 8½x11 paper ISBN 1-56308-491-0

EXPLORING DIVERSITY: Literature Themes and Activities for Grades 4–8
Jean E. Brown and Elaine C. Stephens

Take the riches of multicultural literature beyond the printed page and into the classroom. With a variety of themes, discussion questions, and activities that challenge misconceptions and stereotypes, this book gives students the opportunity to develop an understanding of and an appreciation for their own and other cultures. **Grades 4–8.**
x, 210p. 8½x11 paper ISBN 1-56308-322-1

COOKING UP U.S. HISTORY: Recipes And Research to Share with Children
Suzanne I. Barchers and Patricia C. Marden

Elementary students will delight in preparing their own porridge and pudding; making candles, soap, and ink; or trying out the pioneers' recipe for sourdough biscuits. This wonderful collection of recipes, research, and readings is divided into units that complement the social studies curriculum.
Grades 1–6.
xiii, 187p. 8½x11 paper ISBN 0-87287-782-5

COOKING UP WORLD HISTORY: Multicultural Recipes and Resources
Patricia C. Marden and Suzanne I. Barchers

Take students on a culinary trip around the world and introduce them to other cultures through the recipes, research, readings, and related media offered in this tasty resource. **Grades K–6.**
xv, 237p. 8½x11 paper ISBN 1-56308-116-4

For a FREE catalog or to place an order, please contact:

Teacher Ideas Press
Dept. B66 · P.O. Box 6633 · Englewood, CO 80155-6633
1-800-237-6124, ext. 1 · Fax: 303-220-8843 · E-mail: lu-books@lu.com

Check out the TIP Web site!
www.lu.com/tip